SEX,
SCIENCE,
AND
STEM CELLS

SEX,

SCIENCE,

AND

STEM CELLS

Inside the Right Wing Assault on Reason

Congresswoman Diana DeGette
with Daniel Paisner

THE LYONS PRESS
Guilford, Connecticut

An imprint of The Globe Pequot Press

10/08

The Lyons Press is an imprint of The Globe Pequot Press.

Designed by Sheryl P. Kober

Library of Congress Cataloging-in-Publication Data

DeGette, Diana.
    Sex, science, and stem cells: inside the right-wing assault on reason/ Diana DeGette, with Daniel Paisner
        p. cm.
    ISBN 978-1-59921-431-3
    1. Human reproduction–Political aspects–United States. 2. Birth control–Political aspects–United States. 3. Abortion–Political aspects–United States. 4. Embryonic stem cells–Research–Political aspects–United States. 5. Embryonic stem cells–Research–Moral and ethical aspects–United States. 6. Embryonic stem cells–Research–United States. 7. Stem cells–Research–Political aspects–United States. 8. Stem cells–Research–Moral and ethical aspects–United States. 9. Sex instruction–Political aspects–United States. I. Paisner, Daniel. II. Title.
    HQ766.5.U5D44 2008   2008012812
    616' . 027740973–dc22

Printed in the United States of America

10 9 8 7 6 5 4 3 2 1

To my daughters
Raphaela and Francesca

POLITICS is the art of
looking for trouble,
finding it everywhere,
diagnosing it incorrectly
and applying the wrong remedies.

—GROUCHO MARX

CONTENTS

ACKNOWLEDGMENTS

Thanks to all who helped with this endeavor. To Dan Paisner for helping me find my voice. To Mel Berger for his dogged faith in the project. To the crew at Globe Pequot, including Gene Brissie, Gary Krebs, Inger Forland, and Justin Loeber, for their commitment to getting this message to the world. To my intrepid staff, especially Lisa B. Cohen and C. Shannon Good. To John Shosky and Darlene Hooley, who encouraged me to write the book and then looked over my shoulder throughout the process. To my family for their steady support, especially my sisters Kathy and Cara for their wise comments on the draft. And most especially to my husband, Lino, for more than twenty-five years of political advice, proofreading, fact-checking, moral support—and for always, always being with the program.

WHAT IN GOD'S NAME . . . ?

Politics and science have had an uneasy alliance for centuries. This is understandable, perhaps unavoidable. Even to call it an *alliance* is to invest the relationship with more points of connection than it deserves. By its very nature, politics reflects the status quo, as governments seek to establish mores that reflect the general society instead of trying to move the laws into uncharted areas of scientific exploration. Science is a much more fluid, unpredictable business. Researchers need to do their work in an unfettered environment, without restraint or agenda or expectations.

In 1633, to cite perhaps the most notorious example of the age-old conflict between science and state, the Catholic Church placed Galileo under house arrest for having the temerity to suggest the Earth revolved around the sun. At the time, Galileo's startling thesis upset the traditional view of the Earth as the center of the universe, around which everything literally revolved. It also infuriated Pope Urban VIII, who issued an order demanding that Galileo recant his theories of heliocentrism because they contradicted the Holy Scriptures. When Galileo refused, he was swiftly punished and his books were banned from circulation.

In our more enlightened age, politicians have been slow to mandate vaccines and fluoridated water because of the public's presumed lack of understanding of the scientific method, and fear of the unknown. The annals of public policy in the United States are filled with examples of shortsighted decision-making based on fear and assumption, while the cupboard is somewhat bare when it comes to examples of forward-thinking initiative built upon the scientific method. Contemporary politicians often point with pride to their willful ignorance of science and claim to stand apart and immune from a rational reliance on scientific fact. They set this out as a good thing, by the way.

There are very few scientists in our U.S. Congress, which these days is filled with lawyers who are taught to argue any side of an issue rather than look at cold scientific reality. Worse, politicians have developed the unseemly tactic of distorting science to their own advantage—and, lately, to the advantage of their friends, supporters, and political allies. Consider George W. Bush and his administration's deliberate misrepresentation of environmental science to make the case throughout his eight years as president that climate change does not exist. The president's intractability on this issue infuriated the scientific community and struck most thoughtful Americans as maddening and absurd.

"Climate change?" Bush seemed to say, covering his ears to the evidence at hand. "*What* climate change?"

Legislators who actually care about science might have seen the president's stance as a harbinger of things to come—or they might have chosen instead to join the Bush faithful and look the other way, while the rest of us were left to scratch our heads.

Bush's refusal to acknowledge climate change was one of the first signature moments of his presidency—and one of the first signs of his lack of respect for scientific fact. There would be many more to come. After his inauguration in 2001, despite a widespread consensus among scientists, President Bush didn't simply ignore the scientific basis for climate change. He took things one step further and denied that climate change had been established at all, presumably under the deluded thinking that if he said something wasn't so in a strongly worded statement, people might believe him. He then declared that more study was needed and referred the matter to another group of "scientists"—specifically, to scientists employed by industries with a financial stake in the issue or appointed by the White House to special commissions established to debunk climate change as some crackpot theory. Congressional leaders subsequently insisted on treating all resulting opinions equally and for years equivocated on climate change without taking any policy action. This inaction, of course, benefited the donors and supporters of the Republican majority in Washington, while our environmental picture continued to darken.

The schism between politics and science is only heightened when you add religion to the mix. This, too, is understandable. American schoolchildren still study the Scopes case of the 1920s, during which the teaching of the scientific theory of evolution was actually put on trial. You'd think we might have learned a thing or two since then, and for a while it appeared we had. During the ensuing decades, a national consensus formed around the teaching of evolution in the public schools, and the controversy over the origin of the species was finally put to rest. Or so it seemed, until Ronald Reagan was elected president and evolution was made a political issue all over again—essentially because powerful evangelicals willed it so. President Reagan and his advisors never forgot that the coalition that placed them in the White House included vocal Christian conservatives who summarily rejected the scientific principles of evolution and believed instead that the Earth was literally created in seven days.

The Reagan conservatives thus began a crusade to establish the teaching of creationism in the public schools as a plausible scientific alternative to evolution—and because of the might of the Reagan White House and the broad reach of the far right, this type of thinking seeped back into our curriculums and across our cultural landscape. We went from conviction to science and then all the way back to conviction, all in the space of a half-century. From local school boards to the United States Congress, the proponents of creationism presented their theory as scientifically based and thus worthy of discussion in the public schools. They dredged up so-called experts to argue that the "science" of creationism had as much merit as the "theories" of evolution. They spoke with the voice of authority and drowned out the voice of reason.

Finally, in 1987, the U.S. Supreme Court determined that "creation science" was not a scientific principle after all and ruled that it could not be taught in the schools. But this did not dissuade the religious right. I'm afraid it takes more than a Supreme Court ruling to derail a right-wing steamroller. Following the high court's decision, religious conservatives simply repackaged creationism as "intelligent design" and went about trying to convince political institutions that scientists had at last discovered a viable, fact-based alternative to evolution that was still somehow based on the idea that the Earth was formed in biblical terms.

These right-wing extremists even republished their old creation science textbooks, substituting intelligent design for creationism and continuing on their determined course. It was an almost unconscionable breach of the public trust, not least because these views had already been dismissed and discredited in the court of public opinion as well as in the highest court in the land.

To this day, these efforts are still being challenged in the courts, and the final chapter on this controversy has yet to be written. There remain scores of influential elected officials in Washington, in state legislatures, and on local school boards around the country who continue to regard the Bible as some sort of infallible historical text—and they're not going away any time soon. To be sure, the crowded primary field of 2008 Republican presidential candidates included several hopefuls who proudly stated that they did not accept the theory of evolution.

In my fifteen years in elected office, I have had a first-hand view of the politicization of science by the Republican Party and the religious right. At times, it has been a frustrating view; at other times, it has been downright frightening; at all times, it was impossible to ignore. I was elected to the Colorado legislature in 1992 and to the U.S. House of Representatives in 1996. In all my years in office, I never served in the majority party until the Democrats won control of Congress in 2006. For those trying to establish sound public policy based on scientific fact, those years before the Democratic victories in 2006 were low points.

Back home, they call part-time legislators, like those who serve in the Colorado General Assembly, *citizen legislators.* When I was sworn in to that body in 1993, I served with a broad cross-section of Colorado's citizens, including former State Senator Mary Ann Tebedo, who said on the floor of the State Senate: "Statistics show that teen pregnancy drops off significantly after age twenty-five."

No kidding.

In my first year in the State House, I learned up close just how worked up the religious right can get about sex and science. As part of Public Health Week, the Denver Department of Public Health set up a display in the State Capitol on AIDS prevention that included information about condoms. Deeming this information too licentious for visiting schoolchildren, my colleague State Senator Bob Schaffer (currently a candidate for the U.S. Senate) took it upon himself to confiscate the brochures.

Heaven forbid that visiting teens might stumble onto a discussion of safe sex!

When I was elected to Congress, the cast of characters became a little more colorful and a little more powerful than in the Colorado State House, while the stakes grew much, much higher. In Colorado, I was working in a body making laws affecting only one state, but now I was working on laws that affected every American. In Washington, I was fortunate to be appointed to the Committee on Energy and Commerce as a freshman member of Congress, and I have served there since. Energy and Commerce has broad jurisdiction over anything relating to the Commerce Clause of the U.S. Constitution, including energy, health care, the environment, consumer protection, and many other issues ripe with potential for the politicization of science. For my first ten years on the committee, I sat through debates where my colleagues railed against scientists who had found that mercury in drinking water created health risks, that climate change was an increasingly threatening reality, and that teenagers were particularly at risk for becoming addicted to smoking. But the real firepower was targeted at health care and scientific research.

Over time, I realized that the politicization of science by the Republicans and the religious right was at its most insidious over any issue relating to human reproduction. This brought me to the inevitable conclusion that too many of our elected officials are simply incapable of thinking rationally about sex. I could think of no other explanation. The disconnect was so transparent that some of our older male politicians couldn't even talk about any aspect of human sexuality without biting their lips to avoid snickering like schoolboys. There was a general and widespread discomfort in talking about sex, except in the form of bawdy jokes passed around by some of my male colleagues. This type of behavior combined with a biblical standard of conduct to make any real dialogue on these issues especially difficult.

From trying to limit the forms of birth control available to women, to issuing federal grants to religious organizations to persuade couples undergoing in vitro fertilization techniques to surrender their unused frozen embryos for "adoption" by infertile couples, the denial of science has extended throughout the executive and legislative branches of government and torn at the fabric of our future. It colors appointments to presidential commissions and agencies and impacts the use of funding limitations for international aid for HIV/AIDS prevention. It has resulted in the United States spending hundreds of millions of dollars for abstinence-only sex education programs, despite numerous studies that have established such programs don't work and are not supported by most Americans. It even permeates the reauthorization of the State Children's Health Program—where, tellingly, the most recent version of the bill allowed states to give insurance coverage to a fetus but not to a pregnant woman.

Why is it important for politicians to rely on science when formulating public policy? Well, it's basic. If we want to fund rational programs that work, we must ensure that they are based on facts—not gut instinct, and certainly not ideology. Otherwise, we will waste the taxpayers' money, and worse, we could do real harm. I call this political malpractice, and it is based on the oath all doctors are required to take before practicing medicine: *First, do no harm.*

Scientific fact is arrived at through use of the scientific method: observation and description of an event, formulation of a hypothesis to describe the event, use of the hypothesis to predict the occurence of other events, and independent confirmation of the experiments. The scientific method is necessary to preserve order in our world and at the same time pursue sound public policy. If we made decisions on the efficacy of certain drugs or treatments based solely on hunches or opinions, we'd be back in the Middle Ages, when alchemy supplanted the scientific method and patients died as a matter of course. If we relied on guesswork rather than scientific calculations when building dams, the dams might break and drown the downstream residents, as often happened before the advent of modern engineering. If we based our views of climate change on the weather this year rather than collecting and analyzing long-term data, we might as well base our climate change discussion on *The Old Farmer's Almanac*.

I'm not alone on the side of science, I'm happy to report. A Union of Concerned Scientists poll in September 2004 noted that 84 percent of Americans believe the federal government has an important role to play in scientific research, and two-thirds strongly believe that science should be insulated from politics.

Too often, the politicization of science brings with it a legislative stalemate that has given new meaning to the term *politically incorrect*, whereby a political decision is so alarmingly and disarmingly wrong that it confounds most right-minded people. For example, the National Right to Life Committee recently opposed my bill to ban reproductive cloning, which most Americans oppose, because it did not also ban so-called therapeutic cloning, which most Americans who understand the distinction wholeheartedly support.

I'm proud—or, I should say, no longer ashamed—to state that we can now debate in my committee a women's health bill involving the prevention of breast or cervical cancer without smirks or giggles on the Republican side of the aisle. But we still can't debate any of these issues without the religious right interjecting false claims and ridiculous assumptions involving sex. The right wing continues to claim that the risk of breast cancer increases following an abortion, even though studies have conclusively demonstrated no such correlation. The same legislators argue that young girls should not be inoculated against the human papillomavirus (or HPV), which would effectively eliminate the most common type of cervical cancer, because the eleven-, twelve-, and thirteen-year-old girls receiving the inoculation might somehow decide to become promiscuous once they had been vaccinated against a disease they'd never even heard of and might not contract for another forty years. The conservatives have conjured up an ailment they call *post-abortion syndrome* and point to it as yet another argument against abortion, even though the mental health community has never recognized such a condition. And they resist a measure to include Plan B birth control—also known as the morning-after pill—in the formulary kit carried by medics on the front lines in Iraq, because our troops are not supposed to engage in sexual activity, and because having Plan B available might turn our American military women into harlots.

When I tell some of these stories to friends and colleagues, they look at me as though *I'm* the one who's got a couple of screws loose. They know, for example, that the religious right seeks to outlaw late-term abortion procedures, but they're unaware that the same political figures also object to birth control—which, of course, *prevents* abortions. They know that the religious right denounces embryonic stem cell research, but they don't know that the same people also believe that the more than 400,000 frozen embryos that are in storage from past in vitro fertilization procedures and are typically discarded as medical waste should be considered as "pre-born" babies and donated to infertile couples for "adoption." They know that Congress appropriated more than $15 billion for international AIDS relief and HIV awareness, at President Bush's request, but they are shocked to learn that the money is being distributed in large part through religious organizations opposed to birth control, organizations that refuse to teach the use of condoms as a component of HIV/AIDS prevention.

In my experience, the citizens of this country have no idea of the systematic perversion of public policy and the misdirection of billions of taxpayer dollars in the name of God—for programs that at best don't work, at worst jeopardize public health, and in almost every case appear to cut against the will of the majority of Americans.

But these are the types of absurdities I've witnessed for more than ten years, and I mean to shine a light on them in these pages.

Before sitting down to write, I went back and checked the public record. It's all there: the late-night debates on the House floor over birth control, the committee hearings where members railed against young women, the missives from religious right organizations to keep scientific discussion out of the public realm. I'm not talking about divisive wedge issues. I'm talking about issues such as birth control, disease prevention, and fundamental medical research; issues where there is a strong public *and* scientific consensus; issues where the religious right has hijacked the public policy of this country.

To my knowledge, no one has systematically exposed the right wing for politicizing sex and science so thoroughly that it is hampering public health and basic scientific reason—and that's what I've set out to do here. Perhaps I'm more aware of the great divide between reason and unreason on these matters because I work with health care issues. In addition to my work in Energy and Commerce, I serve as co-chair of the bipartisan Congressional Pro-Choice Caucus, so I end up leading the fight against these Luddite proposals. I'm also the co-chair of the bipartisan Diabetes Caucus, so I fight for expansion of ethical scientific research on that front as well.

And it's not just me. Even though I work in these areas, the politicization of any topic related to reproduction is well known but little discussed in Congress. It's almost like we've become so conditioned to deal with this craziness that we've accepted it as a way of our political life—like a Congressional Stockholm Syndrome. There's a pattern to it, I've come to realize. Often, when a bill comes to committee on the floor, a little buzz will start that typically means the religious right has found a way to interject its social policy into legislation seemingly unrelated to these topics. Soon, little pockets of pro-science leaders will form on the House floor and a delegation of Democrats will cross the aisle to find our few remaining Republican allies. Strategy sessions will be held to figure out how to stave off disaster. The leadership will be alerted, and invariably I will pull together a group to head up an informal whip effort. And somehow, some way, science and reason will prevail.

Or, not.

This happens every few weeks when Congress is in session. Readers would not believe some of the ideas we've thwarted in this way—and that's the central objective of this book, to call attention to the inexorable subversion of science at the hands of religious conservatives.

In order to let readers know how I got to this place in my thinking, I believe it's necessary to share a little bit about me. After all, if I mean to be your tour guide through the mess and morass of Capitol Hill on legislative issues relating to the touchy subjects of sex and human reproduction, then you need to know where I'm coming from.

You need to know that I'm not the Child of Satan that my conservative critics have painted me to be.

You need to know that I believe in God, attend church regularly, and even sing in my church choir, at Montview Presbyterian Church in Denver.

You need to know that I consider compassion and justice to be central to my Christian values and believe that advancement of ethical science is wholly consistent with those principles.

You need to know the depths of my commitment to sound public policy and proactive legislation that not only accommodates the scientific breakthroughs that will shape our future on this planet, but also encourages them.

You need to know these things and more, if I'm to be any kind of credible witness to the strange goings-on in our nation's Congress. And so I'll begin these pages with a brief rundown of my family background and a sketch-memoir of my call to political office. I'll talk about my first months in office as a state legislator and the rude awakening I got when I tried to pass a bill requiring right-to-life protestors to leave a clear path of at least eight feet to allow patients unrestricted access to abortion clinics throughout Colorado. I'll talk about my daughter Frannie's diagnosis of Type 1 diabetes at the age of four, and how that diagnosis changed not only our family dynamic and the course of Frannie's life, but also the course of my political career. And I'll talk about my various attempts to overturn President Bush's shortsighted 2001 executive order to restrict embryonic stem cell research to a precious few existing stem cell lines.

It all begs the same question: What in God's name are these people doing? Why does the religious right try to limit scientific advances where they relate to human reproduction? There are no easy answers here, but I've come to believe that the most extreme (and, frequently, the most influential) right-wing advocates seek a country that comports with their view of the Bible. If it was up to them, they would not only outlaw abortion altogether, but also all forms of birth control except the rhythm method and abstinence. Embryonic stem cell research would have no place in their society, although I don't know what they would do about in vitro fertilization. Yes, IVF gives thousands of couples the opportunity to have children, but it also creates thousands of unneeded embryos that are eventually destroyed. In the Christian fundamentalist worldview, if our public policy reflected their values, God's will would be done. Sex would be reserved for marriage and be limited to procreation, and AIDS and other sexually transmitted diseases would magically go the way of the dinosaur.

Sound preposterous? Maybe, maybe not. But I have not arrived at these conclusions hastily. In my view, there is simply no other explanation for some of the nonsensical policies the American people have been saddled with under President Bush and the previous Republican majority in Congress.

Here's my idea: If we can return to a rational, science-based exploration of sex and human reproduction, it seems to me we can enact policies that will benefit millions of people around the world. We can restore common sense to the discussion of everything from funding decisions to disease-prevention strategies that will help us progress.

It's a big deal, don't you think? After all, this *is* the twenty-first century.

ONE

WHERE I STAND

My family has lived in Colorado since the turn of the last century—and I believe the strong Western values in my DNA have shaped my political ethos. Coloradans are proudly independent and value common sense and fiscal discipline. We don't necessarily care about political labels, which is one of the reasons why I think I've always worked well with my Republican colleagues. And we strongly believe that the government should not interfere in people's private lives, so you could say there's a strong libertarian bent to our lifestyle and philosophy.

Not only are we Westerners, in the traditional sense of the American West, but my family also embraces the diversity of cultures in the American immigrant tradition. My maternal grandfather's family, the Rosenais, were Russian Jews who immigrated to the United States following one of the pogroms in Poland. They arrived in Cleveland but soon moved to Denver so my great-grandmother could be treated at National Jewish Hospital for a respiratory problem. By this time, the family name had been Americanized to Rose while the family had settled on the west side of Denver, which was a real melting pot in the 1920s and 1930s. There, my grandfather, Alex Rose, met my grandmother, Anna Delaney, one of five children of Irish Catholic immigrants. Like many immigrants to the West at that time, the Delaneys had come to Denver to work on the railroad—and, as it turned out, the railroads would play a critical role in my family history.

My maternal grandparents were probably the biggest influences on me when I was growing up. I credit them with my tolerance, my idealism, my righteous indignation—which I suppose means my right-to-life critics can blame them as well. The West Denver of my grandparents' youth was filled with diversity: Hispanics, Jews, Irish, Italians. A great many immigrants came to Denver to work on the railroad, seek a better life for their families, and find better opportunities for themselves. It was the post-war version of the Gold Rush. You could find your way if you were willing to work hard. That was my grandfather's story. He worked for the Rio Grande Railroad. He worked his way up from messenger at age fifteen to vice president of insurance when he retired at sixty-five. He was probably one of the railroad's last fifty-year guys. We'd always been told that he was born in Cleveland, but after he died we found his passport, which revealed he was from a small town in Poland. It was a stunning revelation to his family, but it was the typical immigrant story in those days. You came to America and buried your past. Even my mother didn't know her own father had been born in Poland.

When my grandparents arrived on Denver's west side, it was socially unacceptable for a Jew to marry a Catholic. But they were in love. Still, this was not necessarily enough for their own parents. My grandfather's mother lived to be almost ninety, and she never accepted my grandmother. After they married, my grandparents looked back on the tension that surfaced in their families over religion and decided to let their children choose their own faith—a fairly heretical approach to child-rearing back then. My mother became a Catholic. Her only brother became a Methodist. My siblings and I were raised big-time Catholic. We went to Catholic school and attended church every Sunday. But we also attended

2

Passover seders with my grandfather and our family friends. My mother raised us to be comfortable attending any church or observing any ritual. That same sense of diversity and acceptance has been passed down to my generation: I am now a Presbyterian; one of my sisters is Episcopalian, and another remains a strong Catholic; my two other siblings are nonreligious.

Like most immigrants, my grandfather was a Democrat. That much was clear. My grandmother, too. It was the party of inclusion, the party of opportunity. Regrettably, their party loyalties were never discussed around our family dinner table, but this was who they were and what they believed.

My father came to Denver from San Antonio. His stepfather was also a career railroad guy, and he worked for Southern Pacific. Most of my father's family hailed from the Great Lakes region. They were German and French Canadian, mostly, which put us all over the map and all over the gene pool. My paternal grandparents were also Democrats—so I had that going for me on both sides, even if it would be some time before I could appreciate that fact.

I was born on a United States Air Force base in Tachikawa, Japan, so you might say I arrived on the scene in service to my country. My parents had gotten married after only a three-month courtship (they met at the Lowry Air Force base in Denver), which might have explained their eventual incompatibility. We returned to Denver when I was still an infant, and that's where I grew up, in an apolitical family. I've always thought that my parents were so busy making a life for themselves that they had no time for politics. I don't know what that explains, but I think it's worth noting because sometimes a seed can flourish in untended soil.

My dad was an architect by training and began his career in Denver upon his return from the service. My mom was a home-maker. That is, until my parents got divorced. After that, my mother became a kindergarten teacher. Being a good Catholic wife, my mother used the rhythm method, which resulted in five children born within six and a half years. I am the oldest. My parents divorced when I was eleven, and I have always joked that if they hadn't quit getting along I would have been the oldest of fifteen. My mother loved being pregnant and having babies and toddlers around; maybe that's why she was such a good kinder-garten teacher later on.

So there I was, growing up in the 1960s in a tolerant religious environment that at the same time did not include any politi-cal discussion or social awareness. There was never any talk in our household about social issues, or change, or race relations—which strikes me now as odd because Denver was at the same time reflecting some of the same social upheaval that was taking place in the rest of the country. Corky Gonzales and his Cru-sade for Justice supporters were agitating in the streets for Chi-cano rights. The Federal Court was ordering the Denver Public Schools to desegregate, causing enormous racial tension and unrest in my community. I was, however, wholly unaware of any of these events at home.

What I took in about the rest of the world came mostly from television. When Martin Luther King Jr. was assassinated, I was transfixed. I was ten years old. I can still remember the televised images from the civil rights movement, which were being played over and over during coverage of Dr. King's funeral: the dogs being trained on protestors by the police, the fire hoses aimed at teenagers marching for equality, the freedom riders being hauled off buses and beaten. I took in these images and wondered how it was that I hadn't known about any of it before the assassination of the great civil rights leader. Even at ten, I came away thinking I should have known *something*.

As soon as I learned about the civil rights movement, I adopted it as my own. Dr. King's legacy was an inspiration, and as I watched his funeral on television—just as the procession was embarking from Ebenezer Baptist Church—I decided I wanted to become a lawyer and work for social justice.

Specifically, I wanted to be a storefront lawyer. There was a show on television I used to watch called *Storefront Lawyers,* and each week the main characters were out there fighting for change. It was my absolutely favorite show. I told everybody I wanted to be a storefront lawyer. I'd never heard the term before I saw the show, and now it was all I wanted. It fit neatly into this picture I'd quickly developed of me working for social change. My grandfather encouraged me in this; he told me I should work hard to achieve my goal, so that's what I did.

By this time, life at home had become chaotic. My parents were divorced. My mother, who had been the quintessential stay-at-home mom, was now forced to go to work. And, as the oldest, I was pressed into service, helping with the little kids and the housework. Despite these demands, however, I remained focused on my idea of becoming a lawyer. I had always been a good student, but where I really kicked it up a notch was in student activities. I became captain of the debate team, president of the drama club, copyeditor of the newspaper. I still had no interest or involvement in politics—I was single-minded and focused on my goal of becoming a storefront lawyer.

I attended South High School in Denver, like my mother. South was a large urban high school, and there was no real focus on preparing students for college. My guidance counselor actually told my father he was surprised that I was thinking of college at all, even though I had just been named Outstanding Senior Girl by the school's faculty. My family couldn't afford to send me to an out-of-state school, so I applied to only one school: Colorado College in Colorado Springs. Luckily, I was accepted, because I didn't have much of a backup plan.

I studied political science at Colorado College—and came into my own as a true academic. My grandfather was always talking to me about how to put myself in a position to accomplish my goals, and now my father re-entered the picture and echoed the same advice. One of the great sadnesses of my life is that my grandfather didn't live long enough to see me through law school. He died when I was in college, but I think he knew that's where I was headed. Everybody around me knew I was going to law school. And sure enough, that's where I landed. For a while, my only concern was how to pay for it—until one of my professors told me about a full scholarship program in public interest law at New York University School of Law, known as the Root-Tilden program. It seemed tailor-made, so I applied and was accepted.

I arrived at NYU in the fall of 1979, carrying two suitcases and wearing a pair of bell-bottomed jeans that were at least a couple seasons out of fashion. I'd never been to New York City, so the prospect was a little intimidating. My dad flew to New York with me, to help me get settled.

When we got to Manhattan, I took one look at all the tall buildings and called my mother and announced, "I'm coming home."

She said, "You can't come home; you have a scholarship."

I didn't like New York at first. Everything seemed too big, too noisy, too dirty . . . too much. I lived in Hayden Hall, the old law school dorm. The walls were streaked with grease, and my window looked onto a brick wall with steam blowing up from a vent.

I thought, I can't possibly live here.

My roommate was a twenty-seven-year-old from New Jersey. She seemed positively ancient to me at the time. The first week of law school, she went through my wardrobe piece by piece, felt all the fabric, and told me which items I could wear at which times of year. She thought I was such a rube I wouldn't know when or where or how to wear my own clothes. I might have been a season or two out of step in terms of fashion, but I was no fool, so I determined to move out of the dorm at the first opportunity.

Several weeks later, I was still looking for another place to live when my ancient, pushy roommate asked if I could turn the pages of my book more quietly. Her reason? I was turning them faster than she was turning her own pages, she said, and my brisk, confident page-flipping noise made her think I would do better on our exams.

I thought, I can't possibly live with *her*.

By second semester, I'd moved into an apartment on the corner of Bleecker and Thompson streets in Greenwich Village and came to love New York and NYU. The early 1980s were an exciting time to be in the city, and I had a front-row seat to the end of a social era. It was right before the AIDS epidemic, so there was a big club scene in the village. The spirit of free love was still in the air, most notably the spirit of free gay love, which to a nice Catholic schoolgirl from Denver was certainly eye-opening. There was a lot of crime in New York at that time. The city was pretty dismal and dirty, but I loved it. The streets pulsed with a real sense of urgency and purpose. I always tell people that NYU law school was my finishing school, because I'd grown up in a sheltered family environment, cocooned from what was going on in the rest of the world, and now here I was, thrust into the mix alongside all these progressive, caring, engaged, *interesting* people.

The students I'd hung out with at Colorado College weren't exactly the most political bunch. They were fellow debaters, mostly, which usually meant they were as comfortable taking up one side of an issue as another. Even though I studied political science, our own political leanings were never discussed in class. If I had to slap a label on my undergraduate experience, I'd say that the Poli Sci department at Colorado College was a rather conservative environment, and yet it was as an undergraduate that I started reading the great political philosophers, everyone from Aristotle to Hobbes. It was through their writings that I started to realize I didn't share the same point of view as my professors. I began to consider where I fit on the political spectrum. Then I arrived at NYU law school and realized that nearly everyone there was far to the left of me. This made sense, of course, once I started to think things through. I was there to study public interest law, in a program surrounded by others looking to act in the public good, so it was inevitable that the school would attract a liberal student body.

I found my political voice at NYU, only I don't think I recognized it as "political" at the time. I knew only that I was out to change the world. My plan was to become a litigator and to pursue impact legislation like all those storefront lawyers I used to watch on television. It all tied in to the civil rights movement, and the images that had been burned into my mind with the assassination of Dr. King. I was going to challenge all those old, tired laws, like Thurgood Marshall and his legal team had done in *Brown v. Board of Education*. I was going to make a difference. I never stopped to think that I was perhaps thirty years too late for that kind of thinking and that few people were making change through impact litigation any more.

I became involved in student politics by accident. Even though I was on a scholarship, I needed a part-time job to earn spending money. I saw an ad for a typist posted in the student lounge, so I applied. It turned out that the job was for the Student Bar Association, the student government of the law school—and soon I became enmeshed in the nuances of politics at the student government level.

Point of view is everything, I quickly realized. What seems radical to one person might appear conservative to another. It all depends on where you stand, and no matter how far to the left I stood there were people standing far to the left of me. The 1960s were over, but the NYU student government was still protesting—over the working conditions of the school clerical and maintenance employees, over the law school calendar (which scheduled finals after Christmas, thereby discriminating against students who had to travel far distances to be with their families), over the size of our activities budget (which I now realize was equal to the budgets of some small cities). Let's just say we did a lot of protesting. We used to stage rallies and walk-outs. It was the first time I'd experienced the thrill of publicly taking sides on an issue, although there were times, I can now admit, when we took ourselves a little too seriously.

I enjoyed the political activism so much I was soon elected vice president of the Student Bar Association and became president in my third year. My tenure as president taught me that sometimes being irritating is the only way to get action. We had many complaints on my watch, mainly centered around the law school's repeated delays in opening a new student dormitory. I'm sure now that Dean Norman Redlich and Associate Dean Franklin Moore were annoyed at our unannounced arrivals at their offices to demand timely completion of various items on our punch list, but to our credit I'm not sure the students would have had housing during my third year if we had not been extremely vocal about getting the dorm finished by the first day of school.

I met the man who would later become my husband, Lino Lipinsky, during our first year, and we became close friends. In fact, he was my campaign manager when I ran for SBA president. We were both dating other people at the time, so our relationship was purely platonic until our third year. That summer, we each broke up with our significant others, and our friendship turned to romance when we got back to school in the fall.

On the face of it, Lino and I were totally different. We still are, in many ways. He was a native New Yorker, and I was from Colorado. He was on *Law Review,* and I worked on the prison law clinic. He was bound for Wall Street, and I was headed for a storefront. He was the yin to my yang—or vice versa. We balanced each other out. Although our career paths seemed to point in different directions, our political views were decidedly similar. He was fairly progressive and from a much more political family than mine. He also recognized the importance of public interest work, but he offset that with a practical side—the need to make a living. Between the two of us, we thought we had it all figured out.

I moved back to Denver the day after graduation. I knew that as a public interest lawyer, it would be nearly impossible for me to afford to live in New York. What I didn't know was that if you weren't on the East Coast or West Coast, there were few jobs in public interest law. That's still true to this day. So I headed back to Denver without a job, and I made a big deal out of it before I left. I was the student speaker at our graduation ceremony in Carnegie Hall, and by then I relished the idea of being thought-provoking in a public forum. So I gave a somewhat controversial speech. I stood up in front of all those people and said, "I don't have a job." Everyone was horrified, because NYU was and remains a top-ten law school, where all but a handful of graduates go on to prestigious jobs. But I wanted to use the platform to tell this newly minted group of lawyers, their generally well-heeled families, and the law school faculty and administration that we were not making enough of a commitment on the societal level to serving the underprivileged and to doing public interest work.

Back in Denver after graduation, I landed a job in the Appellate Division of the Colorado Public Defender's office, making $21,000 a year. The bad thing about handling nothing but criminal appeals is that all of your clients have been convicted. They're in prison and the odds are stacked against you. We worked our butts off, researching the case law and putting together brilliant briefs, and then the state Attorney General's office would file a two-page response that essentially said, "Well, your client was found guilty, as stated, and there might have been an error in the handling of his case, but even if there was it was a harmless error." And then the court would affirm the conviction. We were beating our heads against a wall.

Lino and I kept up our long-distance relationship. I invited him out to Colorado to visit me over the July 4th weekend in 1982. He was in New York, studying for the bar exam, and he needed the break. He'd never been west of Ohio, so I thought I would give him a real Colorado experience. I took him on the Aspen-Vail loop, the full Rocky Mountain tour. One thing about Colorado, it makes a great first impression—and a great lasting one, too. At one point, he turned from the majestic scenery toward me and said, "You know, I could live out here." I thought, okay, maybe the altitude has gotten to him, but then a couple days later, after he'd had time to adjust to the thin air, he still felt the same way. He moved out to join me one year later, and he's a total Coloradan now.

Meanwhile, the criminal appeals job turned out to be grueling—and frustrating. I think I handled about sixty criminal appeals during my stint at the Public Defender's office, and most of them didn't go anywhere. By this time, Lino and I had gotten married, and he had found a good job with a law firm in Denver. I started thinking I wanted to work in one of the Public Defender's trial offices because I could do more to help my clients and also develop my legal skills by trying cases in court. Trouble was, there weren't any openings in the Denver metro area, which meant I would have had to relocate to Grand Junction or some other trial office in rural Colorado. I thought, *What's Lino going to do there?* He'd already given up his position at that New York firm to come out to Colorado, and I couldn't ask him to quit Denver for an uncertain job in some sleepy outpost.

So I shifted gears and signed on with a small civil litigation firm that had several Root-Tilden graduates from NYU and a reputation for doing good public interest work. The trouble this time was that six months after I arrived the firm announced it would no longer pursue public interest cases, which left me in a bind. That was the sole reason I'd joined the firm in the first place. I went home and told Lino the news. I said, "I've got to quit." And Lino just said, "Okay." That's the great thing about my husband—then and still. He's always with the program.

The only thing to do, I thought, was to start my own firm, so I hung out my shingle. I rented an office in a building with three other solo practitioners. It was just like my own little storefront office, at long last. After a while, I was joined by Sue Kauffman, who ended up working for me for more than ten years, becoming my secretary, paralegal, confidante, honorary aunt to my children—and, eventually, my congressional aide. It was a struggle at first to drum up business and to keep ahead of my bills, but I had some good experience as a litigator at this point. My name was out there, along with what there was of my reputation, and enough business trickled in to keep the place running when I was just starting out. I handled a lot of court appointments. I did some criminal work. I represented prisoners without pay for the American Civil Liberties Union. I was a volunteer attorney for the Sierra Club, working on wilderness litigation. And then I had some small commercial litigation clients. That's how I paid the rent. It was a good mix of cases that kept me interested and solvent, and at the end of each day I was content in the knowledge that I was helping people who couldn't always help themselves.

Along the way, I rekindled the passion for politics I'd developed at the Student Bar Association. Back home in Denver, it resurfaced as a fun civic hobby, but it quickly became more than just an outside interest—it became a *passion*. It started almost as a lark. I volunteered to work on Richard Lamm's last gubernatorial campaign. Folks in Colorado know Lamm from his three terms as governor. Folks elsewhere remember his unsuccessful 1996 bid for president as a candidate of Ross Perot's Reform Party.

After growing up in an apolitical household, the idea of working on a campaign was intriguing. Plus, I thought it would be fun. (That's one of the things readers need to know about us political types: We actually think campaigning is fun.) I was a little late to

13

the party, though. Because it was Governor Lamm's third campaign, they didn't need another volunteer and so they redirected me to a state legislative campaign. I didn't know the first thing about state politics, but I fell in with a group of political activists from central Denver. We all worked tirelessly for a candidate for the State House of Representatives named Norma Edelman. All my friends on the campaign were young and idealistic, and I fit right in with them. We were out to change our little corner of the world, together, one election at a time. Norma's campaign manager was a young lawyer named Mike Johnson, and it turned out Mike had some political ambitions of his own. He revived a group called the Denver Young Democrats and became its president. I became vice president, and I started getting more and more involved. Mike ran for the legislature soon after, and I managed his campaign. Unfortunately, he lost. But by then I was hooked on politics.

It's funny, the way you can go from zero to sixty in no time flat. That's how it was with me and politics. I grew up knowing nothing about how our government worked, nothing about how elections were won or lost, nothing about getting an issue out there and talked about—and, certainly, nothing about making laws or setting policy. But now that I was hooked, I couldn't turn away from it. In 1983, I joined Federico Peña's first campaign for mayor of Denver. That campaign was a real magnet for our Denver Young Democrats group. Peña, of course, won that election and went on to lead the redevelopment of Denver's new airport and was eventually named to two Cabinet positions under President Bill Clinton—transportation secretary and energy secretary. Before Peña, we had this ossified mayor who'd been in office for fourteen years, William H. "Mayor Bill" McNichols Jr.

Mayor Bill had badly mishandled a snow removal crisis following the Christmas blizzard of 1982, which was about the worst thing a Denver mayor could do, and Federico stood in contrast as a young, fresh-faced innovator. The race resonated for me on a personal level, as it did for a lot of young voters in Denver. I became Federico's District 9 campaign co-chair—one year out of law school, with just a couple months' worth of experience on Norma Edelman's campaign—and for the first time in a long while I felt I was truly making a contribution.

Federico's headquarters were in an old tire warehouse downtown. It was a big open space, with a glass-walled conference room where the campaign's advisory committee met. Every time I went into the office to pick up my precinct list or my phone list or to collect new literature, I'd walk by this conference room and notice that most of the people on the other side of the glass wall were male. The women were the ones on my side of the glass, doing all the work, while the guys were sitting inside this fish bowl of a conference room mostly shooting the breeze and sometimes talking strategy. It didn't bug me too terribly much at first, but I certainly took note, and it bugged me a little more each time I passed that conference room. One of these guys was my co-chair of the District 9 field operation, and he didn't put much time into door-to-door campaigning.

A light bulb went off in my head. Up until that time, it never occurred to me to run for public office, but I caught myself thinking, *If these people can do this, then so can I.* And as the years went by, I thought about it more and more. I talked about it with Lino, and with my good friends. I started to think that if I really wanted to work for social change, and if the time for impact litigation on a big scale had come and gone, then it was time to look for another way. Yes, I was helping people in my little law office, but I was helping them in an isolated, one-person-at-a-time sort of way, not on any kind of global basis. If I ran for office, I realized, I could make public policy on a large scale.

Now, a lot of people I've known since high school tell me they knew all along I'd run for office someday, but that was never my objective until this epiphany in Federico Peña's headquarters. Personal ambition wasn't exactly a motivator for me. I was in this to do good work—to help people, to make a difference. I sound like a walking cliché, I know, but that's really how it was for me. I thought I could accomplish these things doing public interest law, but that was turning out to be one frustration on top of another, so now I found myself on the political sidelines, waiting for the right opportunity to run for a position where I thought I could make a difference.

It took some time for an opportunity to present itself. I didn't want to run for office just for the sake of running for office. I wanted to win—and I wanted a position where I could make a real impact.

Fast forward to 1990. In the years after Federico's election, I continued to work in my private practice and to volunteer on various campaigns. I remained active in local politics. We were also starting our family. Our daughter Raphaela was born in 1989, and soon enough I was back at work, keeping my law practice afloat, and back at my political meetings with my daughter in tow, asleep in her infant carrier. Raphaela has been attending strategy sessions and community meetings since she was three weeks old—ever since the Denver Democratic holiday party in 1989, where our congresswoman, Pat Schroeder, gave our new baby her first Christmas tree ornament.

Every ten years, legislative districts are redrawn to reflect population changes, and in 1991 word came down that there would be redistricting in central Denver, where we lived. Denver was losing population, which meant we would lose a seat in the State House. My state legislator was a crusading consumer advocate named Jerry Kopel, who had been in office for twenty-two years. We learned that the Republican-controlled legislature was planning to combine Jerry's solidly Democratic district with that of a retiring Republican legislator. This put a distinctly Republican spin on the newly drawn district, which of course worried the Denver Democrats. The last thing we needed was to lose a seat in the legislature, where we had been the minority party for more than twenty years. There was a lot of strategizing and theorizing and good old-fashioned politicking as we tried to adjust to the change in landscape. I suspected that Jerry might opt for retirement rather than risk losing to a Republican after such a distinguished career. No incumbent likes to be forced into new territory like that, after a long, successful term in office. You always want to go out on top if you can, on your own terms, and I had a hunch Jerry was thinking it was time to leave the legislature.

I had been the treasurer of Jerry's previous two campaigns, so I met with him to discuss my plans—which, of course, were tied to his. I said, "Jerry, I think you're a wonderful legislator and I would never suggest you retire, but I just wanted you to know that if you did decide to step down I would run for your seat."

Then I went around to all of the Democratic precinct committee people, the activists, and the party leadership and told them the same thing. I wanted to put the word out that if Jerry did announce his retirement, I would consider running, so I might emerge as an obvious candidate. I was thirty-four years old, and at this point a veteran of the local political scene, so I guess you could say I was at least somewhat politically savvy. I knew my place was in the state legislature, where I could draft and, I hoped, pass legislation that could have a positive impact. And the timing seemed exactly right. A generation of would-be successors had waited for Jerry to retire and had moved on to other challenges as Jerry won re-election year after year. People don't wait around forever—not for a part-time position that paid only $17,000 a year.

As it played out, Jerry did decide to retire in early 1992, and I was well-positioned to make a run for the District 6 seat. I didn't have the field all to myself, though. There was a guy who wanted to run for the seat, and frankly he had more experience than I did on the local political scene, but he viewed the State House seat as a stepping-stone for the Attorney General's office. He was a partner at a big law firm, and it was clear he didn't really want to be in the legislature. I had the temerity to get on the little mall shuttle we have downtown and march straight to his office to stake my claim. I didn't make an appointment. I just showed up, and when I got there I said, "Look, I don't think you should run for this just as a stepping-stone. The constituents in District 6 need a representative who wants to work for them, not one who'll be looking at statewide office in two years. This is a position I really want. This is a job I know I'll be good at. I'm going to run one way or another, but I'd like to have your support."

Somehow, I convinced him not to run, and I managed to gain the party's nomination without a primary. The Republican candidate didn't face a primary either, so we were duking it out well before the general election. Because of the redistricting, it was the hardest-fought race in the state that year. I raised and spent more than $53,000, and my opponent, Clarke Houston, raised and spent about the same. Together, this huge sum established a record for the most money spent in a Colorado legislative campaign, which makes me chuckle now. My first Congressional run cost more than $1 million, and it's not uncommon to see Congressional races in which each candidate spends $2 to $3 million.

In the end, I managed to win over 53 percent of the vote. I was thrilled. Lino was thrilled, too, because he knew what it meant to me, to finally have the opportunity to craft legislation that could change people's lives. I was elected in November 1992 and sworn in the following January. My daughter Raphie was three years old. I still had my law practice, only by now I had moved to my own suite of offices and sublet some of the space to other lawyers. Somehow, I had to cover my overhead, carve out four months or so to accommodate the 120-day "part-time" legislative session, and still find time to be a mom. It was a lot to juggle, but we managed. Very quickly, I became of counsel to another firm, which was essentially an office-sharing arrangement because I thought it would be easier than maintaining my own office on such a split schedule.

After I was sworn in, Lino and I looked at each other and realized that if we wanted to have a second child it made sense to do so in an odd year so I wouldn't have to campaign while I was pregnant. This was how we began to think of our lives, in two-year election cycles. And so our second child, Francesca, was born in November 1993, just six weeks before the State House convened in January.

Absolutely, it was a lot to juggle—a newborn, a toddler, a law practice, and a position in the state legislature. People often ask me how I did it, and I tell them I don't remember a lot from those years. But for the first time in my young career, I went to work each day thinking this was exactly what I was meant to do.

TWO

THE BUBBLE BILL

The very first piece of legislation I wrote as a brand-new state legislator was so deeply rooted in common sense I worried it wasn't bold enough, that it wouldn't send a message—and worse, that it would have no effect if it passed.

I'd been looking for some way to make a mark on an issue that was important to me and my constituents. It was 1993, and I kept coming back to the fact that Colorado had been the first state to adopt liberalized abortion laws, and yet it had been twenty-five years since we had passed any pro-choice legislation in the state. That's a long time. A great deal had changed in those intervening years. A persistent anti-choice mentality had taken hold in the governing Republican Party, and I was looking for a way to reinforce the all-important point that the state of Colorado still supported a woman's right to choose and to send a message to the religious right that our views would still be counted. The day I was elected, I promised myself that I would draft practical, real-world legislation wherever possible and help people use those laws in their daily lives, so it was only natural that I wanted my first bill to fulfill that promise.

I had some help on this. As soon as I was elected to the legislature, I started hearing from all kinds of pro-choice groups about various initiatives. As one of the few young female legislators in the state, it was only natural that some of these groups reached out to me—because gender lines can be as strident as party lines on certain issues. At the same time, I reached out to friends, colleagues, and like-minded constituents and engaged them on the subject. I tried to listen to every point of view. I had all kinds of big ideas, and yet the consensus seemed to be that I shouldn't try to codify *Roe v. Wade* or undertake any sweeping initiative that might merely put an exclamation point on existing policy. People were encouraging me to think small instead of big, because you can sometimes cover a lot of ground with small steps, even though I worried that the message wouldn't be heard if these steps were too small.

Meanwhile, there was a groundswell of protest taking place outside health care clinics across the state. The protestors were targeting women seeking abortions, although the clinics served all kinds of patients, ranging from women with cervical cancer to women getting checkups. It was a serious problem—not just in Colorado, but all around the country. The protestors would block people from entering these clinics; they'd scream at them and spit at them and otherwise intimidate them. It was an ugly, ugly situation—real bullying tactics, in full force—and the unintended effect was that people who had no position or role in the abortion debate were staying away from these health clinics. In some larger cities, such as Denver, there were pro-choice volunteers to help escort patients through the dizzying maze of protestors. At other locations, women had to get past this intimidating gauntlet on their own.

To me, this wasn't a pro-choice issue so much as a freedom-of-speech and public civility issue. That's the great thing about the legislature, I quickly realized. You can approach a big problem in a sidelong way and still take a bite out of it. Chuck Schumer, who was in the U.S. House at the time, had recently introduced a clinic access bill, so I decided to draft a more direct bill at the state level. Because the protestors got into people's way and actually prevented access, I wanted to require them to stand back a certain distance from patients entering or leaving a clinic. That's all I wanted to accomplish. It was a small, straightforward approach to a complex issue, but it seemed like the right thing to do—and, as I suggested, it allowed me to take an indirect swipe at the pro-life contingent, which had lately been out in force. I drafted the bill with my friend Mike Feeley, who was a brand-new state senator. Together, we rookies were going to make a difference on a matter of real importance to the people in our state, because we were going to go at it in a practical way.

We thought it was a no-brainer—a tiny little baby step over which everyone would surely agree.

I soon found out that in the Colorado legislature, there is no such thing as a no-brainer. There's always some surprise or other. Also, we had no budget for staff, so we were on our own. Mike and I were both lawyers, and we drafted the legislation ourselves with a mandate to each other to keep it simple. Remember, we were thinking small. We just wanted to get something done, on an attainable scale.

As I wrote earlier, I had been a volunteer lawyer for the ACLU, so I knew about people's First Amendment rights. At the same time I couldn't help but think that protestors did not have a constitutional right to block people from accessing health care. The one didn't follow from the other. So the first thing we did was determine a reasonable distance the protestors should be required to stand back from a clinic entrance to clear a path for the patients. Mike and I actually stood over the desk where we were working and stretched out our hands, to measure the distance between us. We thought two people, double-arms' distance apart seemed about right. From that distance, you can still make yourself heard, you can still make your argument and hold out a brochure to a patient, and there would still be a clear path for people to pass. It would allow the patients to go in and do what they needed to do, and it would allow the protestors to stand slightly off to the side and do what they felt they needed to do. The rights of both sides would be protected. It came to about eight feet, so that's what we drafted.

We chose our words carefully, trying to anticipate a legal challenge. (Always, I would learn, you must anticipate a challenge.) We wrote that it was unlawful for protestors to "knowingly approach" within eight feet of another person, without that person's consent, for the purpose of passing a leaflet or handbill, displaying a sign, or engaging in oral protest, education, or counseling with that person. We applied this standard to any person or persons within one hundred feet of the entrance to any health care facility in the state.

It was the first bill of its kind in the country. I remember thinking how remarkable that was, because it seemed so basic: it was such an obvious response to a pervasive problem, and I was surprised no state legislator had come up with it before. At the same time, I didn't think it was any kind of big deal. It was just a common courtesy, rooted in common sense, and I fully expected it to slip quietly into law and allow us to do the right thing, for once.

Sure enough, it turned out to be one of the biggest pieces of legislation in Colorado that year. Usually, you can see opposition coming a mile away, but here it pretty much blindsided me. Who could be opposed, I wondered, to something so reasonable, so practical, and so fair to both sides of the abortion debate? And besides, I wasn't asking my new colleagues to take a stand on the choice issue. I wasn't asking Coloradans to forsake their right to assemble and protest. I was just asking them to be reasonable about it—to go about their business on either side of this issue and to treat each other decently as they did so. But I misread the room on this one. The right-to-life activists argued they should be allowed to get as close as possible to patients to make themselves heard. They wanted to get right up in their faces. The pro-choice folks wanted unfettered access to health care for all patients, including those seeking abortions. And there was our little bill, stuck somewhere in the middle, trying to serve both ends in a sensible way.

For the first time, I was made cruelly aware of the power of elected office—and, by extension, by the power of the opposition, specifically the religious right. Here I'd been thinking that if my ideas were ratified by my colleagues and in the court of constituent opinion, we'd be able to make some changes. If not, we would not make those changes—but at least we would try. At least we would get a dialogue going. I hadn't counted on any personal attacks against me and my family along the way, but that's just what happened. And these attacks would continue for a number of years on a variety of pro-life issues—all on the back of this initial bill, which set me up as a target.

We have a very active right-to-life group in Colorado, which likes to protest at every opportunity. Some of the protestors are a little strange. One guy dresses up like Abraham Lincoln and rides his bicycle past our house. He's tall and thin and wears a tall top hat. I believe he has many complaints, including an objection to a woman's right to choose. I've got no idea what his other beefs are, but he appears around town protesting on a fairly regular basis.

He often walks up and down the pedestrian mall in Denver at lunchtime, speaking his mind on the issues of the day.

Once I had stepped out in front on this issue, I became a God-less, soul-less menace to these people. They started picketing my home, almost from the moment the bill was introduced. It was frightening at first. I would be sitting on my living room couch reading the paper, only to look up and see twenty or thirty people pile out of cars and vans with large posters and signs and start marching around my house—on the public sidewalk, of course, because these folks know the legal limits to residential protest in Denver. Their signs were practically the size of billboards. At least that's how they seemed to me. They featured monstrous photo blow-ups of what were supposedly aborted fetuses. The photos were clearly doctored, but it was a little unnerving, to say the least. They also brought video cameras and megaphones, so they could yell things like, "Stop killing babies, Diana!"

Our routine became to draw the blinds, move to the back of the house, and call the police. In the beginning, I was tempted to step outside and talk to these people, but then I realized this would only inflame them. I didn't think it was possible to have a thoughtful conversation with a group of people shouting at you through megaphones. So I just tuned them out, turned the television on at high volume, and tried to convince my kids nothing was wrong—that all the other mommies had protestors show up at their homes and call them baby-killers. I'd close my eyes and think back to our student government protests during law school and hoped to God we didn't sound as nutty as the people outside my window.

When the protestors first started showing up, we were concerned about the effect all of this noise and tension would have on the other families on our block. Luckily, Lino and I had a terrific bunch of neighbors. Our immediate next-door neighbors, Dan Reilly and Mary Kelly, had the best attitude. Dan actually had some fun with it. If he was home, he'd step outside and turn his sprinkler up full blast so the water sprayed into the middle of the street. For good measure, he'd walk across to our yard and turn on our sprinkler, too. This put a literal damper on the marchers on the sidewalk.

Our other neighbors were also supportive, and occasionally one would go out and try to talk sense to the protestors. The local police department would send a patrol car. Either we'd call the precinct if we were home, or one of our neighbors would summon an officer. That was the drill. One day, when Denver was on watering restrictions because of a drought, the responding officer got out of his car and walked over to Dan. The police officer looked at Dan, and then he looked at all the hoses and all the water and all the protestors. He was silent for a moment. Then he turned to Dan and said, "Sir, I can't tell you how to water your lawn."

Once, the protestors cornered two young girls who lived down the street from us and told them that, if I had my way, their mothers would have aborted them. Those poor little girls were simply terrified. Can you imagine anyone saying that to kids in the name of God?

Another time, we were trying to leave for a vacation and the protestors were blocking our driveway. We put the kids in the back seat and threw a blanket over them, because we didn't want them to see the altered posters and we certainly didn't want the protestors to taunt our kids. It was quite a scene, with us backing up our loaded station wagon while the police held the protestors at bay, with my little children huddled in the back seat under a blanket. It was a harrowing moment for a young mother—not to mention a young legislator—and it still feels as if it happened yesterday. I told the girls to stay hidden, but Frannie poked her head out from under the blanket and stole a look. She was just a toddler and was curious, so of course she looked.

A couple days later, we were hiking in the mountains and Frannie quietly came up to me and said, "Mommy, I've been having nightmares about those monsters on the posters."

By monsters, she meant the doctored images the protestors carried on their picket signs.

I said, "Don't worry, honey. Those monsters aren't real."

I shuddered to think how these people could go out of their way to disturb little children. I thought their stated mission was to protect children, not to traumatize them. But I guess I missed one of their memos.

When I arrived in Washington, I assumed that the anti-choice protestors picketed all the pro-choice members of Congress. But then I was on the floor one day, and I happened to mention to a colleague that the protestors had been at my house in Colorado again that weekend. This person had no idea what I was talking about, so I explained. He couldn't believe it. Nothing like this had ever happened to him, and he'd never heard of it happening to any other member of Congress either. So I started asking around. No one I asked had ever had protestors appear at his or her house.

I thought, *Hmmm, how did I get so lucky?*

Say what you will about these right-to-lifers, but they certainly know how to organize and mobilize and make their presence known. They'd bring their kids with them. Sometimes, they'd invite the so-called Lambs of Christ, young adults born after *Roe v. Wade*, who would join the protest. These demonstrations may have started with my first piece of legislation, but they didn't end there. And they didn't end with me. At one point, the Colorado right-to-lifers started picketing abortion providers' houses. They camped out on the sidewalk in front of these doctors' homes and set up lawn chairs, and even barbeques, as if they were having a party. Then they would shout at the doctors and their children and their neighbors. They screamed ugly, hurtful things through megaphones or portable loudspeaker systems, and it got to be quite intrusive and quite awful.

Inevitably, the protestors targeted some of the more liberal churches in my district. Easter, for obvious reasons, became like a busman's holiday for these people. One of their traditional protest locations became St. John's Episcopal Church, where they picketed the churchyard while the children rolled their Easter eggs on the lawn.

Mother's Day was another highlight on the protestors' calendar—also for transparent reasons. I always wondered what their strategy sessions were like, sitting around some conference table, deciding that Mother's Day would be an appropriately symbolic day to make their rounds.

One year, I was scheduled to give an update on the congressional agenda at my church, Montview Presbyterian. Some well-meaning soul placed an announcement in the community calendar of our local newspaper. The protestors arrived to let the parishioners know what they thought about my position on choice. They surrounded the church and began taunting people as they arrived. The ushers and church elders had to go outside, both to restrain the protestors from getting too close to the churchgoers and to restrain the churchgoers from giving the hecklers hell for disrupting a place of worship on a Sunday morning.

Finally, the service started, and during the Prayers of the People the minister stretched out her hands and said, "Oh Lord, we pray for those outside exercising their First Amendment rights. Please grant them the gift of tolerance."

I thought, *Boy, have I found the right church!*

Now, whenever I speak at my church about the upcoming congressional session, nobody calls the newspaper, and I've started to think that some of my feisty fellow congregants are a little disappointed when the protestors don't materialize.

I also wonder what these people think they're accomplishing, because the protests are so extreme and yet my community—my neighbors, my church—is completely supportive of me, my family, and other pro-choice activists, even if they might disagree with my position on this or that issue. My constituents have come to look on these people as a nuisance, like flies on the windshield. Over time, I think the protestors realized their message was falling on deaf ears, because they started turning out less frequently and in less force. After a while, I started joking with the kids that I missed having them around. They still turn up, from time to time, and a part of me feels like bringing out a plate of cookies for them and saying, "Hey, where have you guys been?"

The last time they came was after President Bush vetoed my first stem cell bill, and by this point we had many new neighbors since I drafted my first piece of legislation with Mike Feeley. This time, one of the neighbors came up to me afterward and said, "Diana, why can't something be done about this?"

I said, "Because they have a First Amendment right to protest. They're not breaking any laws, although I don't really understand what they think they're achieving. They're just annoying."

Oh, my neighbors must love us! Now, every time a new

family moves in on our street, I go over with a little welcome gift to introduce myself. I tell them what I do for a living. Then I tell them about the protestors. I say, "It's nothing to worry about. If these people show up, just call 911 and tell them you're our neighbors and the police will come right over."

How's that for a neighborly welcome?

Lately, the protestors have been targeting builders and contractors. It's a nationwide effort, actually, and it's terrible. Whenever Planned Parenthood announces plans to build a new facility, the anti-choice zealots find out who the builders are and go and picket them. Of course, these construction workers are not public figures. They're not prepared to deal with this. They're just doing their jobs and trying to feed their families. Plus, over 80 percent of what Planned Parenthood does has nothing to do with abortions. They offer obstetric and gynecological care, cervical and breast cancer screenings, prenatal care, and general medical services, so these protestors are mostly barking up the wrong tree. What is really disturbing, though, is that these craven tactics are occasionally effective. The protestors don't just picket: They harass and intimidate and scare these good people. Protestors recently succeeded in shutting down construction of a new building in Texas—and, as I write this, Planned Parenthood is building a new facility in Denver, and the anti-choice contingent has started picketing the *subcontractors* on this one.

Getting back to my first big bill, the Republican leadership tried to kill it in committee because they knew it would be difficult to argue against common courtesy once it got to the House floor. That's how it often goes with a controversial piece of legislation that doesn't appear to the general public to be at all controversial. If you don't head it off at the pass, the court of public opinion is usually enough to see it through. But I wasn't content to just take our chances and hope for the best. I enlisted the help of two Republican freshmen, Russ George and Bill Kaufman. Like Mike and me, Russ and Bill were lawyers. We served on the Judiciary Committee together. Over and over, they came to me and reported that they had been told by Republican leadership that the bill was unconstitutional and had to be killed. Over and over, I went through the provisions of the bill with them and shored them up. At the Judiciary Committee hearing they stuck with me. The Bill passed committee, after which I turned out to be right: once the Bill got to the House floor, people felt stupid voting against it. The Bill passed the House and got to the Senate floor.

When the Bill went to the Senate Judiciary Committee for a hearing, the chairwoman of the committee, Dottie Wham, a moderate Republican, decided to make a point about the eight-foot restriction. She placed the witness table exactly eight feet from the legislators. The opponents of my bill demonstrated just how close eight feet was when they tried to tell the senators how their speech would be restricted if they stood back.

The bill then went to the Senate floor, where even Bill Owens, an ultra-conservative pro-life state senator who went on to become governor in 1998, realized he had to vote with us. He came up to me on the Senate floor and said, "Diana, I'm voting for your bill because it's just common sense." (Not incidentally, I knew at that moment Bill Owens was running for governor. Such were the vagaries of state politics and playing to both sides of an issue.)

There are 100 legislators in Colorado—35 state senators and 65 representatives—and 81 ended up voting for our bill.

That in itself was a small miracle—one that I would see again in my rearview mirror several years later as we attempted to pass the stem cell bill in Washington, only here we had a Democratic governor who signed it into law. But then came the court challenges. An anti-choice protestor named Leila Hill sued the state of Colorado for allegedly denying her First Amendment rights and her ability to express herself freely on an issue of great importance to her.

I thought, *What planet are these people living on, that they can find something to oppose in such a fair-minded measure?* I even had pro-choice people coming up to me and complaining that eight feet was nowhere near enough. They said I should have made the safety zone twenty or thirty feet wide, because at just eight feet away the protestors could still yell and spit and throw things and otherwise intimidate someone from entering the clinic. Maybe it was enough room to keep the protestors from physically impeding a patient's access, but it was still a big hurdle to get past. I didn't think a wider zone would be upheld as constitutional, and now here was Leila Hill claiming eight feet was too much of a gap for her to get her point across.

Hill v. Colorado got so much attention in the Colorado press that my bill earned a nickname. Right out of the gate, the first piece of legislation I wrote had a nickname. Some reporter dubbed it the "Bubble Bill," because it sought to create a safe zone or bubble to protect patients from protestors, and it caught on. I actually liked the name, because it suggested a shield that could apply both to protestors and patients.

The name stuck, and the bill unobtrusively did its thing. Even with the Hill suit hanging over its head, throwing its constitutionality into question, and even with the protestors who continued to show up at my house, my church, and my office, the spirit of the bill was upheld across the state. People on both sides of the argument respected the intent, and there was a generally positive response from the pro-choice camp, which reported a significant drop in incidents of harassment at area clinics and hospitals.

Of course, this did not mark the end of the Bubble Bill saga. Eventually, through a slow route up and down the court system, the case reached all the way to the U.S. Supreme Court. Although the Colorado Supreme Court had upheld it, the Supreme Court's decision to scrutinize the bill further was troubling. By the time it got to the highest court, I was already in my third term in Congress, but I had kept a close watch on my bill as it bubbled its way to Washington. One of the groups I'd consulted with when I wrote the bill was the ACLU, and lawyers there expressed confidence it would be upheld, along with lawyers from other pro-choice groups. But when it was finally taken up by the U.S. Supreme Court, I got a call from my friend David Miller, who as legal director of the Colorado ACLU at the time had helped me and Mike Feeley write the bill.

He said, "Diana, I think your bill's unconstitutional."

I said, "Gee, David. Thanks for letting me know now. It's kind of too late, don't you think?"

The concern was that our eight-foot restriction could be selectively applied. In other words, it would be difficult to establish criminal conduct if we could not differentiate between an individual approaching a health clinic patient with an admonition on abortion or one sharing a general pleasantry about the weather. How could the law provide for the latter without also accommodating the former? It was an interesting dilemma, one we certainly wrestled with as we drafted the bill, but once again I thought the greater good was being served in the effort to restrict these negative, taunting, intimidating encounters.

I'd followed all these challenges closely as I moved from the state legislature to Capitol Hill, and I carved out some time on my calendar to attend the Supreme Court arguments. I hoped my little law would somehow prevail. As a member of the Supreme Court Bar, I was able to sit up in front. They don't let you sit up front just because you drafted the bill that's being challenged, but I knew there was some reason I bothered being admitted to the Supreme Court Bar all those years ago. In fact, I had never been in the majestic courtroom of the Supreme Court until I attended the argument on my bill. I slipped in anonymously. Nobody knew I had any personal connection to the case. I sat next to two legal reporters who were covering the proceedings, and the whole time I had to resist the urge to tap one of them on the shoulders and proclaim, "Hey, this is my bill."

It was such a quiet thrill, to be sitting directly in front of the nine justices while they were preparing to listen to the oral arguments, to see the highest court in the land consider a law that began as a series of scratch marks on my legal pad, but at the same time I was frantic over the outcome. As a legislator, you want a bill you helped to draft to stand up in court, otherwise there's no point to the whole process.

I was caught in that weird, uncertain space between thrilled and nervous, and the Colorado solicitor general wasn't helping my emotions. He wasn't helping my case, either. The justices were grilling him about how far was too far for a protestor to stand, how close was too close. He appeared tentative, uncertain. Remember, my fear once the case was accepted by the Supreme Court was that the law might be ruled unconstitutional. I kept hearing this and talking myself into thinking we might be all right. Still, I kept thinking, I don't know, it just seems reasonable. It doesn't seem like any kind of undue restriction. I thought the intent, to keep an open access to medical care, was a higher good, but then I watched our solicitor general get pounded by the justices. They started asking him all kinds of hypothetical questions, and he just couldn't answer them.

All of a sudden, I started to lose my confidence.

At one point, one of the justices asked the solicitor general the legislative intent behind the bill, and he couldn't answer. I was so tempted to thrust my hand into the air and shout, "Here I am! I wrote the bill! I can tell you the legislative intent!" But I sat on my hands and held my tongue.

The two reporters sitting next to me had no idea who I was, and I listened in to their back-and-forth comments. One of them said he'd never seen a performance like that before the highest court.

I said, "What do you mean?" The reporter didn't seem to mind or even notice that I had been eavesdropping.

He said, "Well, the solicitor general had it in his grasp and now it's gone."

I said, "Do you think it'll be overturned?" I couldn't believe we might lose this fight in the final round.

He said, "Oh my God, yes."

I thought, *Not just* yes. *It had to be* Oh my God, yes. I thought, *That can't be good.*

I walked out of that courtroom feeling certain that the law would be tossed. I was really, really upset about this, but then I tried to put it out of my mind and move on to all the other pieces of legislation lining up for my attention. A month passed, and there was still no word on a decision, until I received a call on the

House floor from my chief of staff telling me the bill had been upheld by a vote of 6–3. Not just a majority, but 6–3! Even the arch-conservative Chief Justice William Rehnquist agreed that my bill was constitutional. Justices Kennedy, Scalia, and Thomas offered dissenting opinions.

This was a giant surprise—a welcome one, but a surprise just the same. I let out a scream of joy. I had meant to give just a tiny yelp, but the next thing I knew I was jumping up and down and clapping my hands together. My colleagues looked at me like I was crazy, which I guess I was. Somebody asked me why I was so excited, and I explained that the Supreme Court had just upheld my bill.

A couple of people muttered some tossed-off pleasantries, such as, "That's nice," and then walked off quickly. I realized they must have thought it was the Colorado Supreme Court, not the big one, but I didn't chase after them to change their impression, because I also realized that they probably hadn't written groundbreaking legislation, made it law, followed it through the courts, and finally had it validated by the U.S. Supreme Court. I thought, Not too many people had done *that*.

So much for my quiet little bill solving a little problem.

The significant footnote to this bill was that there were only a few arrests made under the new law. The police and prosecutors told me that, following passage of the "Bubble Bill," order was restored to the clinics, and the protestors even took care to back up when patients approached. (If only they took that same care when they showed up at my house!) I took that as a sign that we hit it exactly right. On this one issue at least, they backed down. We had sent just the right message to the pro-choice community and just the right message to the pro-life community. Everyone knew the parameters.

Indeed, the Bubble Bill came closer than any other piece of legislation I helped to write in achieving its precise intent. It allowed patients to move freely in and out of these clinics and, at the same time, it allowed protestors to continue to have a voice and exercise their freedom of speech. And it marked one of the first and only times in my career where I allowed myself a small sigh of satisfaction and thought, *This is why I became a lawyer.*

THREE

MS. DEGETTE GOES TO WASHINGTON

From time to time during my first term as a state legislator, people asked me if I would ever consider running for higher office. The question always surprised me.

By higher office, most folks meant the U.S. House of Representatives, but that was the furthest thing from my mind. I already had the job I wanted. I had my law practice, which was still humming along nicely, thank you very much. I had my two little girls, and my supportive husband. Plus, my congresswoman was Pat Schroeder, who at that point had been in Congress for more than twenty years and was beloved by everyone in Denver, including me. I was actually approached early on by a political friend who tried to get me to run against Pat in a primary, and I said, "Why would I do that? I love Pat. She represents me well."

And she did.

Mercifully, I ran unopposed for re-election to the Colorado State House for my second term. Between juggling our busy household and managing my two (hardly) part-time careers as an attorney and a state legislator, I wouldn't have had time to run an all-out campaign. There were a lot of balls in the air, and it's a wonder I was able to keep them up there. To have to manage a hard-fought campaign on top of all that . . . well, those balls would have all come tumbling down.

Early in my second term, I was elected assistant minority leader of the Colorado State House, which was a great honor. The best thing about it was that it was an election of my peers, so my colleagues must have thought I was doing a decent job—at least the ones on the Democratic side of the aisle. Even the press was positive. The Associated Press named me Outstanding Freshman Legislator—another great honor. I was happy and productive in the State House, passing legislation in the minority party by teaming up with Republicans like Russ George and Bill Kaufman. I even dreamed that in the right political climate I might rise to become the first female speaker of the Colorado House—an honor that ended up going to a Republican after I left.

One of the bills I was most proud of was a strong piece of environmental legislation called the Voluntary Re-Development and Clean-Up Act. The bill was designed to help clean up contaminated commercial properties, like abandoned dry-cleaning establishments and gas stations, by offering various incentives to property owners. I worked on it with the Sierra Club *and* the Chamber of Commerce. The Republican legislature was prepared to kill it—but as Business Affairs Committee chair Paul Schauer said in explaining his support, "I couldn't really go against *both* the Sierra Club and the Chamber of Commerce, could I?"

No, he couldn't. That would have been like fighting Smokey the Bear and General Motors at the same time. This was emblematic of my strategy right out of the gate—to present reasonable bills in such a reasonable way that even our opposition would have a tough time defeating them—and here it worked out for the greater good. The legislation has been enormously successful, and we've cleaned up hundreds of properties because of it.

More important than the honors and the recognition was the fact that I was able to accomplish some of the goals I'd set for myself when I first decided to run for public office—to write purposeful, impactful legislation, and to address some of the difficult issues facing our community in a straightforward, reasonable way. In many ways, they were an extension of the primary goal I set when I graduated from law school: to do sound public interest work. As an outsider looking in, I'd never accepted the notion that party politics and constituent interests could get in the way of good, practical government or reasoned public policy. Now that I was on the inside looking out, I was determined to get past the status quo and the quid pro quo and every other *quo* that undermines so many of our elected officials.

So there I was, liking what I was doing, getting things done, and keeping all those balls in the air and those *quos* at bay. I would have been perfectly content and fulfilled to keep going on this particular course. But then, on November 29, 1995, right after Thanksgiving, I received an unexpected bulletin. It was the day after Frannie's second birthday. Raphie had just fallen, and we thought her wrist was broken, so I took her to the emergency room at Children's Hospital. Thank goodness it just turned out to be a sprain. I hustled her back to the car, thinking I could return her to school in time for lunch if I hurried. I'd left my cell phone in the car in the hospital parking lot, and when I unlocked the door I could see the lights flashing on my phone through the window. Very few people had my cell phone number back then, so I figured the call must be important. I quickly strapped Raphie into her car seat and answered the phone. It was Sue Kauffman, my assistant. She said, "Are you sitting down?"

I climbed into the front seat and said, "I am now."

She said, "Pat Schroeder is retiring."

Sue might as well have told me the sky was falling, it was such a startling piece of news. Pat Schroeder was only in her mid-fifties. She'd been in Congress for twenty-three years. She was young enough and admired enough that she could have stayed on another twenty-three years—and the good people of Denver would have been lucky to have her. She'd never given any public indication that she was contemplating retiring, so of course it never occurred to me that her seat would be up for grabs. Even now that she had announced her retirement, I could not believe the seat was open.

I called Lino right away to get his take. He thought about it for just a moment and then said, "Well, you have to run."

I thought, *That's my husband.* Always with the program. Even when neither one of us is entirely sure what the program should be.

I said, "Are you nuts? Do you know what that would mean? For Raphie and Frannie? For you?"

He said, "It doesn't matter. You have to run. You love what you do, and this might be your only opportunity to do it on a national level. Whoever wins this seat will hold it for a generation. This is the chance of a lifetime."

Realize, this was something we'd never discussed, even in our most private, pie-in-the-sky, "tell-me-what-your-hopes-and-dreams-are-Honey" moments. Yes, I had some influential friends in town who'd occasionally sit me down to talk about my political future, but I never paid too much attention to my political future, not least because I believed my political present was exactly where I was meant to be. And yet even during those "career-planning" conversations, I never even thought about running for Congress.

But there was my supportive, cheerleader of a husband on the other end of the phone, telling me I should run for Congress like it had been my long-held dream. Forget what it would mean for him and his own career. Forget what it would mean for our young family. Forget the upheaval and the aggravation and the uncertainty.

He said, "Promise me you'll think about it."

I said, "You're nuts."

He said, "Just think about it."

So that's what I did. Right there in the car in that hospital parking lot. I turned off the phone and closed my eyes, forgetting for a moment that Raphie was in the back seat. This was the greatest decision I had ever faced in my career. I must have looked ill because after a moment or two Raphie spoke up in a concerned voice. She said, "What's wrong, Mom?"

I said, "Pat Schroeder's retiring."

And Raphie, all of five years old at the time, said, "Congratulations."

I said, "What do you mean, 'Congratulations'?"

"Well," she said, "isn't this a good thing for your job?"

Out of the mouths of babes, right?

I continued to think about it as I drove Raphie to school. The more I thought about it, the more it made sense. I thought, *Even my daughter thinks this is the right move for me, so there must be something to it.* At the very least, I knew, I wouldn't be dismissed out of hand or laughed out of town—important considerations, both. Among my Denver colleagues, I was the senior ranking Democrat in the state legislature. Not the longest serving, but the senior ranking, thanks to my recent election as assistant minority leader. But just like it was with Jerry Kopel's State House seat, people had been lined up for twenty-three years waiting for a chance to represent Colorado's 1st Congressional District, so it's not like I would have the field all to myself. In all likelihood, I'd have to take my place in line and wait my turn.

After I dropped Raphie back at school, I made a beeline for my friend Rick Ridder's office. Rick is a political consultant in Denver and the only person I knew who had worked on a successful Congressional race. I burst into his office and told him the news, which at this early juncture he had not yet heard. Then I said, "So what do I do?"

He said, "What do you want to do?"

I said, "I honestly don't know."

Of course, Rick knew me well enough to figure that if I was ambushing him in his office, asking him what to do, it probably meant that on some level I wanted to at least *consider* making a congressional run. So we sat down and starting making a list of other likely candidates. Very quickly, our list filled his white board. We analyzed it and analyzed it and I finally said, "I think I'm going to think about it."

That was the short-term plan. It was the end of November. The legislature wouldn't be back in session until January. I figured I could take the month of December to decide, although I told myself right there in Rick's office that if I could raise an appropriate amount of money I'd go for it. I set that number at $50,000—a tough number to reach in just one month, especially December, which is typically one of the most difficult months for political fundraising. I think maybe I put such a high price tag on my decision so that I could give myself an easy out if I decided in the end not to make a run.

As it played out, I raised the money, mainly by calling through my Christmas card list. (I bet my friends were happy to hear from me *that* year!) When I looked up from a frenetic few weeks of fundraising, there were six or seven other people mulling a run for the seat. However, there were only three of us still in the mix when we had to file for the primary, and that number finally whittled its way down to two: me, and a popular former city councilman named Tim Sandos. At first, many local activists thought Tim would have a leg up in the race because he had been elected citywide, whereas I had only served my smaller legislative district. Also, Tim had the endorsement of Denver Mayor Wellington Webb, which was a big deal. But I just plowed ahead and ended up winning the primary with 55 percent of the vote—a comfortable margin in a two-person race.

Pat Schroeder weighed in with an endorsement just after the primary, which of course provided an enormous boost heading into the general election. Naturally, if you're hoping to succeed a beloved member of Congress, it helps to be endorsed by that beloved member of Congress. We had a press conference to announce her support, and one of the reporters said, "Boy, those are big shoes to fill," which for good or ill is something I would hear for years and years after I got to Washington. But Pat, as ever, was ready with the perfect comeback. She said, "Well, let's just see about that." Then she took off one of her pumps, handed it to me and said, "Put it on."

Now, a gesture like that could have easily backfired, but I've always chalked it up to good advance work on Pat's part that the shoe fit perfectly. I put it on and smiled for the cameras and said, "I feel just like Cinderella."

My opponent in the general election was Joe Rogers, an African-American Republican Party activist. Joe was a polished orator whose silver tongue camouflaged his conservatism. He had written an op-ed piece attacking attempts to equate gay rights activism with the civil rights movement. Somehow, Joe forgot to mention his party affiliation time and time again during the

1996 campaign, because Colorado's 1st District was heavily Democratic. Still, it's a racially diverse district, so a lot of people thought Joe could win the seat. The *New York Times* even wrote a story predicting that a Republican was poised to succeed Pat Schroeder.

Joe certainly had a way with words. When he was just starting out in politics, he'd worked as Pat Schroeder's intern. At some point during his internship, Pat told Joe in an offhanded way that she hoped he would one day succeed her, which Joe touted in 1996 as an endorsement. She told the same thing to her other interns, by the way. She was just being kind and generous.

In our campaign, Joe earned himself a new nickname: Republican Joe Rogers. We always made it a point to call him that in public. In one of our television commercials, we even trotted out a picture of Joe with the very Republican Speaker of the House, Newt Gingrich, taken during Newt's trip to Denver to hold a fundraiser for Joe. Joe didn't appreciate our tactics, but the voters got the message and I ended up winning with 57 percent of the vote.

The issues I campaigned on were the issues I worked on as a state legislator: women's rights, choice, and the environment. Fortunately, these issues resonated with voters, and with Pat Schroeder in my corner I was a pretty formidable opponent.

My campaign was nearly derailed on September 15, 1996, just one month after the primary, when I got a hysterical phone call from my sister Kathy. My dad had died unexpectedly of a heart attack at age sixty-four, seven years after my mother's death from lung cancer. I suspended the campaign and flew to Florida, where my father had lived at the time of his death, to help my stepmother, Nell, with the funeral arrangements. My dad may have been a Republican, but he was always one of my biggest supporters—even though he made me pass a public-policy quiz before he agreed to give me a campaign donation. I was devastated to lose him and sad that he wouldn't be with me if I made it to Congress, but I contented myself in knowing that he lived long enough to see me clear what was arguably the biggest hurdle in the primary.

It all happened so fast—and to this day I can't remember all of the details of the election. But what I do recall and will never forget is the adrenalin burst of excitement I felt at being elected as a United States congresswoman. It was like a rush inside a blur inside a dream I would never in a million years have been presumptuous enough to have. And yet there it was.

We only had a few weeks between the general election in November 1996 and my swearing-in ceremony in January 1997. There was a lot to take care of. Lino and I briefly considered splitting up our family while Congress was in session, with me taking an apartment in Washington and commuting back to Denver when my schedule allowed, but we quickly rejected that notion. Raphie was six and Frannie was two when I was elected, and there was no way we could be apart so many days each week during those early years. It would have been hard on Lino, hard on the girls, and hard on me. Of course, Lino and I had talked generally about these issues as we tried to figure out what our lives *might* look like if I won the election, but it's a much more urgent discussion once it's a done deal.

And so very quickly we made arrangements to move our family to Washington. There was such a short window between the election and the swearing-in that we had only two days to plan our new lives in Washington. We spent one of those days on a whirlwind tour with a Realtor and ended up renting a house in Bethesda, Maryland. Then I leased an entire houseful of furniture in one hour at a rental store by walking around and pointing and saying, "I'll take that living room, that dining room, that master bedroom. . ." We found schools for the girls, too, even though the entire community was shut down because of a sudden snowstorm.

Lino closed down his law firm in Denver and started looking for a job at a law firm in Washington. We decided to keep our house in Denver, partly on the advice of Federico Peña, who had made the mistake, he said, of selling his house when he moved to Washington to become secretary of transportation. He said, "You'll need a place in Denver anyway, and you'll never be able to buy back in your neighborhood." That made sense to us, so that's just what we did. We found a tenant named Gary Abrams, who had just moved to Colorado to run the Bar Association's continuing legal education program. Gary was more of a house sitter than a tenant. He paid a reduced rent, but in exchange for that reduction he had to move out whenever we came home, which couldn't have been too convenient for him. Still, he must not have minded too much, because he stayed on for years. The kids called him Uncle Gary, he took good care of our house, and it was a workable arrangement all around.

At the time, there were fewer than ten women in Congress with young children, so there was no real roadmap for me to follow. When she arrived in the House in 1973, Pat Schroeder became the first woman with small children to serve in Congress, so this was still fairly new territory. Most members of Congress were older than I was when I was elected (I was thirty-nine), and most of their kids were older than ours, so we had to figure things out as we went along. More to the point, there wasn't a whole lot of time. One of the things they don't tell you when you're running for Congress is that freshman members are expected in Washington right away. For most of us, we've just been through the election of our political lifetimes, and then when you're trying to hire your staff and figure out your life you have to attend an official freshman orientation at the end of November. And that's just the *official* orientation, where you lobby your party leadership for committee assignments. There's also an orientation organized by the Congressional Research Service, and others by the Heritage Foundation and Harvard, to name just three. At these sessions, you're overloaded with documents and briefings and everything you could possibly need to know to hit the ground running. You learn about parliamentary procedure, floor rules, and the meaning of the buzzers telling members it's time for a vote. You walk away with your head reeling.

While we were in Washington for these sessions, we incoming members of Congress were each given a small cubicle to use as a makeshift office. They've got roomfuls of these little cubicles in the basements of the Rayburn House office building—because, of course, our predecessors were still occupying their offices during this interim period. In my case, Pat Schroeder was kind enough to make her staff and office available during the orientation sessions, but that's not always how it goes. In fact, it's not even *usually* how it goes. When an incoming freshman member has defeated an incumbent, the transition is tense and difficult and there's no way the outgoing staff will extend a helping hand. Even retiring members who did not seek re-election are not always so gracious when it comes to reaching out to the new guys.

I was extremely fortunate to have Pat in my corner. She was wonderfully supportive and available during this transition period and continues to serve as a mentor and advisor. She took me to lunch on a regular basis and talked me through the political landscape. She told me that the House of Representatives consists of 435 independent contractors and that I had to learn to work with each one of them on their own terms, through their own perspective. I thought that was a good way to look at it. She told me in a good-natured way that I had no idea what I was getting myself into, and she would send me funny, uplifting cards and notes with simple messages like "Hang in there, Diana," or "Buck up," or whatever was appropriate to whatever was going on at the time. Her notes not only made me smile but made me grateful to have a predecessor so eager to smooth the way.

Staffing was my most immediate concern outside of our own personal family issues—and in many ways it was the biggest deal of all during those weeks of transition. The key position I was looking to fill, of course, was chief of staff, someone to be my point person and right arm to run my offices in Washington and Denver in ways I could not. I kept going back and forth on this one. A sharp, politically savvy young woman named Lisa B. Cohen had worked with me as a consultant on my congressional race. I liked her enormously, and we got along great. She did a wonderful job on my campaign. Like me, Lisa had no Washington experience, and at first we both agreed that I needed an old Washington hand as my chief of staff, which meant I started to look elsewhere to fill this all-important position. Lisa understood—I think she even agreed with me—and I started to think of ways she could stay on in some other role.

Next, it came time to lobby for committee assignments, and I decided to seek an appointment to the powerful Committee on Energy and Commerce, a spot almost always reserved for more senior members. Lisa helped me develop a strategy for getting onto the committee—and lo and behold, it worked! I realized that if Lisa could navigate the nuances of committee assignments she could certainly run my office, so I told her I'd changed my mind and asked her to be my chief of staff. She readily agreed and has been with me now for more than eleven years.

One of my other early hires was another very talented woman from Denver, C. Shannon Good. Shannon first came to my attention as a volunteer on my campaign. She was hard-working, smart, and fearless—so fearless that she once brought me some papers to sign during the only workout I'd managed to squeeze in over the course of my eight-month campaign. Despite that rocky start, Shannon applied for an entry-level position on my staff as legislative correspondent. It's a thankless but essential job that involves drafting responses to the thousands of constituent e-mails and letters and giving tours of the U.S. Capitol. Shannon quickly proved herself to be a rock of common sense and stability, and she has been promoted over the years to legislative director, where she now oversees all the bills and legislation my office handles. She's also ridden point on most of the crazy issues under discussion here.

One of the first tasks facing my new staff during this transition period was to sit me down and press me with questions. Lisa took me aside one day and said, "Okay, what do you want your profile to be as a member of Congress?"

I thought that was a strange question. I said, "I have no idea what you're talking about."

"Well," Lisa said, "what do you want your persona to be?"

The rephrasing didn't help. I still didn't know what she was talking about. I said, "I don't know, I just want to be a really good legislator."

That seemed like a good response, and my newly assembled staff appeared to nod as one, as if to say, "Okay, good, that's settled."

For the life of me, I couldn't think of another reason why someone would seek the job, so I said, "Wait a minute, what other profile is there?"

Lisa responded that there were a lot of other profiles: Some representatives see Congress as a jumping-off point for higher office; some want only to deliver strong constituent services to the people back home; and some had no idea what they wanted.

Lisa was with me for my very favorite fish-out-of-water/ welcome-to-Washington story, which took place the day after my swearing-in ceremony. We were on the way to the airport in our little rental car, loaded with luggage and kids. But on the way we were scheduled to stop at the White House for a photo opportunity to honor the Colorado Avalanche hockey team for winning the Stanley Cup. I'd only been a member of the United States House of Representatives for one day and already it was business as usual. Already, I was going to the White House! I thought, *Well, this is going to be a pretty good job.* Of course, I learned soon enough that whenever one of the major sports teams was honored at the White House after winning a championship, the presidential staff invited members of Congress from the team's district to attend—and here it was, my first day on the job, and it was my turn. I was particularly excited because I happen to be a big hockey fan—and the Avs, our brand-new Colorado team, were of course my favorites.

There were five of us—Lino, Raphie, Frannie, Lisa, and myself—squeezed tight into our subcompact rental car, which was crammed with all of our suitcases. It had been a crazy, hectic, wonderful few days, with no time to sit still or catch our breath—and no time, certainly, to fuss over our wardrobes. The girls were wearing their pretty little dresses again, and we adults were in our business suits, which we had already worn a couple times that week. Our clothes were a little rumpled by this point, but they were the best we had, considering the circumstances.

I approached one of the White House gates and said to the guard at the checkpoint, "Hi, we're going to the White House. They're expecting us."

As soon as I said it I thought it was probably one of the top-ten lamest things anyone had ever said to a White House guard in the history of the United States.

The guard pretended not to notice and very kindly said, "Who are you?"

I said, "I'm Congresswoman DeGette." It was the first time I'd introduced myself in this way, and it was thrilling. It almost made up for the lame approach.

The guard said, "Let me see your I.D."

I reached into my pocket for my brand-new Congressional I.D. It was the first time I'd had to use that, too.

Finally, the guard said, "Just go through the gates, drive up the street a little way, and you'll see another gate. Turn left and go in."

Then he waved us through.

Of course, I had no idea where to go. There were temporary bleachers in place, up and down Pennsylvania Avenue, which had been set up to accommodate the crowds for the second Clinton inaugural. You couldn't really see where you were going when you drove up the street, because you were moving through this canyon of empty bleachers. I couldn't even use the White House itself as a kind of visual marker. Lisa and Lino were no help. We were just inching along Pennsylvania Avenue, which was closed to traffic for security reasons, but that's where the guard had directed us. We were the only car on the street, and we were peering out of the windows, trying to find the magic gate. It was just me and my family and my chief of staff, crammed into this tiny rental car, in our crumpled clothes, rolling up a deserted Pennsylvania Avenue through a canyon of empty bleachers.

We made a strange picture, I'll tell you that.

At some point, a gate to my left swung open, so we took that as a sign and turned into it. Right in front of us was the White House. We pulled over on the driveway and parked right in front of the West Wing. We unfolded ourselves from our seats, stepped outside, and flashed each other pinch-me looks. None of us could believe that we were walking around on the White House grounds, just outside the West Wing, but sure enough that's where we where.

We stood there in awe for a few moments. We said things like, "Oh my God, we're standing at the White House!" Or, "I can't believe it!" Apparently, we said these things loud enough for other people to hear, because as it turned out we were standing right next to an area reserved for broadcast journalists to do their stand-up reports for their evening newscasts. Wolf Blitzer of CNN finally turned to us and said, "Could you keep it down over there?"

For a beat or two, it felt like we were the Washington Hillbillies, and we'd just a-loaded up the truck and moved to D.C. It was a little embarrassing, but only a little. I thought, *I hope I don't ever lose this sense of wonder and excitement and purpose and whatever else it was that I was feeling at just that moment.* I tell my staff and my colleagues all the time that the moment you start to feel jaded as a member of Congress is the moment you should quit, because it really is an awesome responsibility. You're making laws that affect all Americans, setting policy that will help to determine our shared future. You're a part of history. Too often, our elected officials become diverted from that. They get all caught up in their re-election campaigns or overwhelmed by the mountain of paperwork they need to slog through each and every day. They start to worry about their *persona*, the way my staff tried to worry about mine before we even got to work. It becomes routine. But I've tried to keep everything in perspective, and in many ways I'm still that wide-eyed Denver tourist, wandering the White House lawn and stepping goofily into the frame of all those television reporters. I'm just so plainly thrilled to be there at all that I can't believe my good fortune.

Really.

FOUR

CHARTING THE COURSE

The Colorado State House was a tremendous proving ground for a young legislator, especially one serving in the minority, but of course nothing can really prepare you for the U.S. House of Representatives. And it's not as if your new colleagues are welcoming you with open arms. Until recently, freshman members of Congress were expected to sit and observe and keep mostly silent, on the theory that there's no way to *really* know your stuff until you've been on Capitol Hill a good long while. Some senior members have been known to completely ignore new members until they've been there several terms, I guess because it could be seen as a waste of time to teach new members the ropes before it's even clear they'll be re-elected.

I decided early on that this sitting-on-the-sidelines stuff wouldn't apply to me. I wanted to add to the debate right from the start. The freshman orientation program helped. It taught me the rudimentary rules of the House, introduced me to some of the key players in Congress, and encouraged me to figure where and how I might spend my time most productively over the next two years. This was especially important because we were at an unusual crossroads when I came to town, in terms of party politics. The Democrats had been in the minority for only one term; prior to that, we had been the majority party in the House for over forty years. Many long-time Democratic members were still shell-shocked over the loss, so there was nobody for me to reach out to on my side of the aisle for advice on how to operate as an effective member of the minority party.

One of the first tasks facing every incoming member of Congress is to vie for committee assignments. Having never worked in Congress, I had no idea how to obtain a committee seat, much less which committee I wanted. Frankly, with the hard-fought primary and general election, I had given the matter little thought. It came up in a substantive way only once. The day before the election, I was driving to an event in Denver with my campaign manager, Lisa Weil. Lisa had worked in Washington for Rep. Tim Wirth when he had been an influential member of the Committee on Energy and Commerce in the 1980s. As we were driving along, a reporter from *Congress Daily* called and asked what committee assignment I might seek. He wanted to get an early start on his story by calling candidates he'd targeted as likely winners of their campaigns. It was the first time I'd been asked the question by a reporter, and I repeated it to Lisa in the car.

She responded, firmly and without hesitation, "Energy and Commerce."

So I said, firmly and without hesitation, "Energy and Commerce." Then I hung up and turned to Lisa and asked her what the committee did.

Energy and Commerce is the oldest committee in Congress; it was actually established in the Constitution. It has the broadest jurisdiction of any other standing congressional committee, with legislative oversight on virtually all matters relating to energy, food and drug safety, health, the environment, telecommunications, consumer protection, and even major league sports. It cuts a pretty wide swath—and, as such, a seat on the committee is a coveted position. Out of our forty-three-member freshman class, we learned that only one would have a shot at being appointed to Energy and Commerce, one of the so-called exclusive committees. I decided I'd go for it anyway. I immediately set about strategizing with Lisa Cohen on how we might make that happen.

The more I talked to people about it, the more I realized Energy and Commerce was the place to be. It's the main policy arm of Congress. Ways and Means raises the money. Appropriations spends the money. And Energy and Commerce charts the course. Membership on Energy and Commerce would give me an opportunity to start legislating right away. As a freshman member, I wanted to develop a niche, because Pat Schroeder and others told me that if I could develop expertise in an area nobody else was delving into, I could set myself apart from the other 434 members of the House and make an impact. Several helpful staff members told me that no one was working in the area of children's health, which was a critical issue. I had also worked on environmental issues and telecommunications in the State House. For all these reasons, and a few more besides, Energy and Commerce seemed like the right fit.

The first thing Lisa and I did was try to figure out how to pitch myself to be on the committee, and who we had to convince. We looked at the list of incoming members to craft an argument about why I should be the lone freshman chosen. We learned that there were about fifteen to twenty of us angling for a seat, so I decided to stress that I was from the West, that I had legislative experience as assistant minority leader of the Colorado House, and that I was a woman.

I was still refining my argument when I attended the freshman dinner sponsored by Democratic leadership in the Capitol Rotunda—a beautiful candlelight event that made us all pinch ourselves and remind each other all over again that we were now *congresspeople* and that this was the *U.S. Capitol.* Across the room, I spotted the committee's ranking Democrat, John Dingell (D-Michigan). John is the most senior member of Congress; he'd been in Congress since 1955, before I was born. But I couldn't let his seniority intimidate me, so I just walked up to him and said, "Congressman Dingell, I'd really like to be on your committee."

It was a classic, what-the-heck approach.

Happily, John didn't shoot me down straightaway. In fact, he seemed to like my bold approach. He said, "Tell me about yourself."

So I did, and then when I came to the part about me serving as assistant minority leader, he held up his hand and said, "Say no more." Then he turned and walked away.

I thought, I *guess* that went well.

Then I happened to be seated at dinner next to David Bonior (D-Michigan), the Democratic whip. He asked me what committee assignment I was seeking.

I said, "Energy and Commerce."

He said, "What's your second choice?"

I said, "I don't have a second choice." This was a risky tactic, because I could have been put on some committee that would have no interest to me or my constituents, but it paid to be bold at a time like this. (At least, I *hoped* it paid to be bold at a time like this.) If it turned out not to be such a good idea, I hoped I'd still have time to regroup and win a second-choice committee assignment useful to my constituents.

David seemed to appreciate the way I was sticking my neck out, and he continued the conversation. He said, "Why Energy and Commerce?"

So I made the whole argument that Lisa and I had devised, about how they needed somebody from the West on the committee—not West, as in California, but the Rocky Mountain West. "Everybody in Washington thinks the West is anything west of the Mississippi," I explained, and then I started talking about the Rocky Mountains, and the great Southwest, and all the issues that were a concern to my region, including energy and telecommunications. I think I gave poor David far more of an answer than he knew what to do with. And I wasn't done yet. I talked about how Bill Richardson (D-New Mexico), the only member of the committee from the Rocky Mountain region, was resigning to become U.N. Ambassador, and how there were only two women on the committee. I said, "With me, you get another woman and the only Westerner between California and Ohio."

David waited for me to finish, and then he just looked at me. After a beat or two, he removed a small piece of paper from his pocket and wrote something down. Then he put the piece of paper back in his pocket—all without saying anything.

Again I thought, I *guess* that went well.

A couple days later, I was grabbing a sandwich with Lisa in the basement of Union Station when my cell phone rang. It was Debbie Stabenow (D-Michigan), our elected freshman representative to the Steering and Policy Committee, which was in charge of the committee assignments. She said, "Diana, you got it."

I didn't know what she was talking about at first. I said, "What do you mean?"

She said, "Energy and Commerce. You're in."

I couldn't believe it. I thought it was such a long shot that I'd crossed my fingers and put it out of my mind since making my appeals to John Dingell and David Bonior, as well as to other influential members of Congress—focusing instead on other tasks like hiring a staff. Sure enough, I'd been awarded Bill Richardson's spot, so my argument about needing to replenish the committee's Western contingent must have registered. However it happened, that year I was the only freshman member of Congress appointed to one of the three exclusive committees—Energy and Commerce, Ways and Means, and Appropriations—and no rookie has been appointed since.

Because Energy and Commerce has jurisdiction over so many substantive issues with scientific implications, there is room for much mischief by the religious right. Sometimes, however, it's difficult to see how a specific piece of legislation might be co-opted by the Christian conservative agenda. For instance, the reauthorization of the Indian Health Act, which has helped foster preventive health care both on reservations and in urban Indian Health Centers, has been held up in committee for several years. Why? Because the right wing wants to insert language into the bill permanently codifying the Hyde Amendment stipulating that federal money can't be used for abortions, even though that language has been included in the annual spending laws for over thirty years and it only tangentially applies to Indian health.

One of the first pieces of legislation I worked on when I joined Energy and Commerce was a bill that created the State Children's Health Insurance Program—or S-CHIP, for short. Years later, the continuing tug-and-pull over our S-CHIP legislation offered another good example of how the religious right tries to insinuate its agenda into every nook and cranny of government, and how those of us on the side of reason must be ever vigilant to try to keep its influence out of our legislation.

As it turned out, in this one case, a presidential veto made our vigilance redundant, but the episode is worth highlighting here.

Some background: S-CHIP provides health insurance coverage to children of the working poor. It's full health insurance, not just well-child care, and it fills a real need in the system. We hear all the time how certain demographic groups keep falling through various cracks in government, and this was one of those efforts to fill at least one of those cracks. Readers might remember that the S-CHIP bill was up for reauthorization in 2007, and that President Bush vetoed it. What they might not recall was that Bush's veto put a swift end to one of the most absurd drafting twists in anyone's legislative memory.

S-CHIP has now been around for more than ten years, and there's always a big fight over it. Republican critics see it as yet another example of big government overextending itself for a group that, under different circumstances, might be encouraged to pay for the program or service directly. From my perspective, it's a sound, necessary bill for a group of people who, for a variety of reasons, are unable to help themselves. But, as I was quickly learning, my perspective only took me so far on some of these issues. This time around, the Senate inserted language into the S-CHIP bill saying that states could offer insurance that would cover fetuses but not pregnant women. Shannon Good pointed this blind illogic out to me, and together we read the changes over and over. We thought surely we were missing something. How could you insure a fetus but not the mother?

At first, I couldn't think how to respond to such insanity, so I reached out to a trusted friend and colleague on Energy and Commerce who happens to be the unofficial Democratic liaison to the Catholic bishops. I went up to him one afternoon in

September 2007 and said, "You can't believe what they just did in the Senate."

I didn't even have to spell it out for him. He knew exactly what I was talking about. He said, "The S-CHIP language. I know. I heard."

I said, "They're trying to get the same language in the House."

Once again he said, "I know. I heard. It's the craziest piece of public policy you can imagine."

I said, "So what can we do about it?"

He shook his head and said, "Nothing, I'm afraid. It's the top agenda item of the Catholic bishops this session."

I said, "You're kidding me."

He said, "I wish I was. I hope you can figure out a way to keep this language out of the final version, because from a policy standpoint it's ridiculous to give insurance coverage to the fetus but not the mother, and I don't want to have to vote for something so ridiculous."

I said, "If it's so ridiculous, how can you vote for it? Why will you have to?"

He said, "The bishops' top concern is codifying the fetus as a person, and the pro-life Democrats will have to vote for it or risk losing the support of the Right-to-Life Committee."

In the end, we were able to keep the language out of the House version, but it remained in the Senate bill and was ultimately included in the final legislation vetoed by President Bush. I looked on as the language snaked its way to the White House and thought, Well, it certainly makes you wonder . . .

I learned early on that you could write the most compelling, most necessary piece of legislation in U.S. history, but if you couldn't come up with the votes to get it passed, it would never become law. It's Government 101—and yet you'd be surprised how many of our elected officials have failed to grasp this basic truth.

For good or ill, I recognized this phenomenon all the way back in the state legislature, when I passed my Bubble Bill. I went out and counted the votes of both Democrats and Republicans, so I knew the likely result going in. On Capitol Hill, they have a name for this sort of thing: whipping. Nobody "whipped" back in the Colorado State House the way I thought to whip. Nobody whipped with the same precision or zeal. I developed a technique where I would approach the member and ask how he or she intended to vote. Then, as the member watched, I recorded the answer on a checklist. I even bought an official-looking clipboard, so when I checked off their answer it seemed like it was a matter of record. The Republicans held only a two-vote majority in the State House during the 1993–94 session, and yet no Democratic legislator figured out that if she could get all of the Democrats and two additional Republicans to side with her, she could pass or kill virtually any bill. I don't even think I recognized what I was doing as whipping, in any kind of traditional sense. I was just laying the groundwork.

When I arrived in Washington, I found out that the Democrats had a large whip organization, and I decided I wanted to be a regional whip for the House Democrats. I realized that whipping was the only way to pass legislation, especially from a minority position, so I thought it would be a dream appointment.

The Democratic caucus was divided into geographic regions, and each region got together during the first days of the session to make appointments to various standing committees. I'd assumed there would be heated competition for what I thought was such a plum assignment, and I was ready to present my qualifications and state my reasons for wanting the job. But it became apparent that the job of regional whip wasn't exactly the most coveted assignment. To the contrary, ranking freshmen were usually forced to take the job, because their more senior colleagues didn't want anything to do with it. And so when the chairperson asked for volunteers for the position, my hand shot up like the teacher's pet in class.

No one else's hand went up, so the chairperson looked to me and said, "Okay, Diana. You've got it."

The Democrats had only been in the minority for two years at this point, so there was still a kind of *majority* mentality among our group. After forty years in the majority, the Democrats had become accustomed to passing legislation with only Democratic votes.

During one of our first whip meetings, there was a heated discussion about concessions we were being asked to make on an amendment then under discussion. It was a concession that would have made a difference in the lives of a great many people—and most of us in the room were not inclined to bend on it.

At one point, the Democratic whip, David Bonior, asked how many votes we had.

Someone responded, "We've got all the Democrats."

Then I chimed in. I said, "How many Republicans do we have?"

Well, you would have thought I was speaking in tongues. Several people turned and looked at me reproachfully, as if to say, We don't count *Republicans.*

In fact, the Democratic whip organization did not count Republican votes. There had been no perceived need, when we were in the majority, but things had changed. The group had not stopped to consider that, when you are in the minority, you could have every Democratic vote and still lose. You need to go across the aisle and get the other side's votes, too.

In the end, we did not cave on this particular amendment— and, as luck would have it, we won the issue with a large number of Republican votes. Still, it would have been nice to know the vote count before deciding whether or not to negotiate.

After that experience, I started whipping Democrats *and* Republicans on issues I cared about. I developed a reputation as someone who was honest about the provisions of bills, and what my position was, and also as someone who knew how to count votes. After a couple of terms, Steny Hoyer (D-Maryland), the new whip, appointed me floor whip. Along with my regular whip assignments, my job was to be on the floor during key votes to help direct traffic and track votes up until the last minute. No one had done that in recent memory, but I believed it was important. Too often, you'd see one of your colleagues who you knew was in agreement on an issue somehow vote the wrong way or waffle on a commitment. The idea was to record as many votes as possible, even if we ended up losing, to communicate our position to the public. And, sometimes, the extra efforts on the floor were just enough to push a measure through and we could actually win a vote.

At first, Republican members of Congress weren't too happy to hear from me. To be fair, they weren't used to whipping across the aisle either, but soon most of them realized I wasn't trying to snooker them. I was just taking their temperature on issues of mutual interest. Typically, when I whip Republicans, I only target members who might agree with our side on the specific issue under consideration. Most of the time, they're happy to let me know their view, even if they disagree with me.

Two sessions ago, I was appointed one of eight chief deputy whips. Together, we reflect the racial and ideological diversity of the Democratic caucus, and the idea is that we'll be able to work every angle of each issue. We hold strategy sessions on key legislation and oversee the whip effort, but we only whip legislation on which the Democratic caucus has taken a position.

I also do a lot of informal whipping on issues where the caucus has not taken a position. Often, those issues involve a woman's right to choose. Since we don't have a consensus of Democrats on choice, we typically don't canvas positions on these votes. In 2007, for example, a group of pro-life Democratic men approached Nancy Pelosi and the pro-choice leadership on an issue that seemed to suggest a fundamental shift when it was first presented to me. These fellows had always opposed choice legislation, but they had finally realized that in order to prevent abortions you have to prevent unwanted pregnancies. This was a major epiphany as far as the choice community was concerned, and I wanted to do what I could to help my colleagues act on it.

They thought they'd found the perfect way to make their point in the upcoming military appropriations bill. They sought to offer an amendment that would provide Plan B birth control to women in forward positions on the front lines. In a massive oversight, Plan B—the so-called morning-after pill—was not included in the formulary kit our medics carry into battle. I wasn't aware of this lapse until it was pointed out to me by these colleagues looking to gather support for their amendment—so at first I was enraged, and a little confused. Why would you omit the morning-after pill—a legal over-the-counter medication available at any military commissary—from the kits at the front lines? Think about it: You're on the front and something happens, whether it's consensual or not. You want to be able to give that soldier birth control so she doesn't get pregnant, the same way you'd give her a flu shot so she doesn't get sick. The pill may be an over-the-counter medication readily available in the United States, but it's not like you could race over to the Baghdad Rite-Aid and buy Plan B.

I was happy to take this on, because it was another one of those issues that just seemed to make sense. Plus, this was my colleagues' first foray into the sticky subject of sex, and both Nancy Pelosi and I wanted to encourage them. It's not often that you get a bunch of pro-life legislators acknowledging that there might be something to this birth control thing after all.

At the same time, we did not want to lose the amendment, so I started whipping votes. What I found surprised me, and in the end I couldn't guarantee that we could pass the amendment. Some of the responses I received were astonishing. One Democrat said, "Diana, I can't vote for anything that touches on abortion."

I said, "This is not abortion. It doesn't even touch on abortion. This is contraception. There's a big difference. And you have to have birth control if you don't want abortions."

"Diana, I know my district," he reiterated. "I'll get killed on this."

I couldn't believe it. I said, "Do you mean to tell me you're not a skilled enough politician to get the message across to your constituents that birth control should be available to our soldiers on the front lines, so they don't become pregnant? This is an FDA-approved medication we're talking about. You can get it over the counter at any drug store in your district. You can even get it on any American military base. We're not approving or condoning anything. All we're trying to do is get this medication into the drug kits that accompany our troops to the front lines."

Again, he said, "I'm sorry, Diana. I just can't support it."

Regrettably, he wasn't the only Democrat who cowered on this one. I whipped the amendment into the ground, and I could see we wouldn't have the votes we needed to pass it. Ultimately, we advised our colleagues not to offer it, because we thought it would send a terrible message if we offered it and lost—another great advantage to a thorough whip effort. You can still end up beating your head against the wall on some of these issues, but at least you don't have to beat your head against the wall *publicly*.

Very quickly, I realized whipping was an art—and that, for whatever reason, I was pretty good at it. You have to look people in the eye and get a sense of what they're really saying. People grow to trust you. Or, not. A lot of times, a member will confide in you. He or she will say, "This is what I'm planning to do. If it helps you to know, that's fine, but I don't want anybody else to know." If you respect that information, your colleague will trust you to work with her on issues requiring the strictest of confidence.

Once, when I was doing some unofficial whipping in opposition to the ban on so-called partial-birth abortion, I approached one of my male colleagues to discuss the matter. The topic of partial-birth abortion is uncomfortable for almost everyone, and it's radioactive for members in swing districts. This particular colleague was on record as being pro-choice, but he was uncertain about his position on partial-birth abortion. As it turned out, he was uncertain about abortion in general.

He said, "Diana, I just don't like the idea of how they do this procedure."

I said, "Well, number one, they don't do the procedure very often, only when the fetus has serious defects, like the lack of a brain stem. And number two, sometimes they have to do this procedure because it's the only way they can save the life of the mother."

At this point, the conversation took a surprising turn. My colleague said, "I don't know, I just wish they'd do a C-section."

I said, "A *cesarean* section?" I wasn't sure I'd heard him correctly.

"Yeah," he said. "My wife and I had a C-section, and it went really well."

I thought, Hmmm. I hadn't realized husbands were now being operated on as well. And then I thought, This is insane. We're not talking about a wanted birth. We're talking about a pregnancy that's gone horribly wrong, and we're trying to terminate it. I didn't quite know what to say, so I said, "We're talking about two different things."

My colleague looked a little flummoxed, so I decided to leave it alone. I didn't count on his vote, because his vote didn't mean anything to him; he didn't really understand the issue. I wasn't really sure that he *wanted* to understand the issue. In the end, of course, he voted for the ban—and I made a mental note to make double-sure that this member was more fully informed the next time a close vote on a complex issue surfaced on our calendar.

Because of my concern about preserving a woman's right to choose and my experience in the State House with the Bubble Bill, I joined the Bi-Partisan Choice Caucus in my first year in Congress. This caucus had been formed in the early 1990s but had become more active after 1994 when the Republicans took control of the House. Chaired by Rep. Nita Lowey (D-New York) and former Rep. Connie Morella (R-Maryland), the caucus fought repeated attempts by the new Republican leadership to restrict a woman's right to choose. The religious right had decided to fight the abortion battle wherever they could. In fact, during the 1995–96 session, 104 bills containing the word *abortion* were considered by the House Judiciary Committee alone!

When I came to Congress in 1997, I immediately jumped in to help. We were fighting the battle on all fronts, and I helped whip the issues when they came to the floor. These were frustrating fights, because most members really didn't want to talk about abortion, and the leaders of the anti-choice movement in the House were doggedly determined to insert the issue in the most insidious ways. Adding to the frustration was the fact that, while we were fortunate to have 25–30 pro-choice Republicans, we had 30–40 anti-choice Democrats, depending on the issue.

In 2001, Minority Leader Dick Gephardt (D-Missouri) asked Nita to co-chair the Democratic Congressional Campaign Committee, and she realized she couldn't do justice to both that job and co-chair of the choice caucus. So she turned to a longtime warrior on choice issues, Louise Slaughter from upstate New York, and to me and asked us to take over as the Democratic co-chairs. We were honored to be asked and quickly agreed.

Louise and I informally divided up the tasks. She would act as liaison for the outside advocacy groups, and I would lead the whip efforts on choice efforts. This is a partnership that has worked extremely well over the years. Now—with the Democrats in the majority—Louise is the chairman of the important Rules committee, which structures legislation as it comes to the floor, and I am chief deputy whip and vice-chairman of Energy and

Commerce, where many of these bills start. We have a dedicated group of congresspeople who work hard on preserving a woman's right to choose, including Rosa DeLauro (D-Connecticut), Jerry Nadler (D-New York), Lynn Woolsey (D-California), and many more.

My position in the Pro-Choice Caucus dovetailed neatly with my appointment to Energy and Commerce and my growing responsibilities as whip, and left me in the perfect position to witness the systematic subversion of sex and science that would take root under the Bush administration. Little did I know that my front row seat to cutting-edge developments in science and health care was about to pay dividends on a deeply personal level.

FIVE

FRANCESCA

Sometimes life throws you a curveball, and how you hang in there and hit that curveball determines everything that happens next. In my case, the curve wasn't really thrown at me; it was thrown at my daughter Francesca. But when you're a parent, you tend to take your hits right along with your children.

Frannie was diagnosed with Type 1 diabetes when she was four years old. It was early spring 1998. I had been sworn in for my first term as a member of Congress in January of the previous year and everything was still brand-new and upside-down. The inevitable fallout from such a move was we didn't really know anyone in town. We didn't know the doctors or the hospitals; we had no support system in place; we didn't even have a pediatrician in the area—just our regular pediatrician back home. Truth be told, I didn't have a whole lot of time to worry about this sort of thing. Raphie was enrolled at Bethesda Elementary School, Frannie was attending a Montessori program, and I had a part-time college student to pick up the kids from school and watch them until we got home. It seemed to me an adequate base of care; Lino and I could divide up the rest. On the medical front, we took the kids in for their regular check-ups when we were home in Denver over the summer and crossed our fingers that they didn't get too sick in the meantime, while I went to work each day and tried to make some kind of sense of the senselessness of some of my new colleagues.

Out of nowhere, Frannie started wetting the bed, which of course struck us as unusual for a four-year-old. She'd been potty-trained for years; we thought we were past that. She also became really, really crabby, and we started to notice she was drinking lots of water. We told ourselves that it was nothing serious. Like most parents, we were in a small pocket of denial at first. Neither one of us had a history of diabetes in our families, but we knew the symptoms. In the backs of our minds, we must have put two and two together on this, but at the same time we dismissed the answer. We thought our child couldn't have such a serious disease, all of a sudden, out of nowhere.

This denial went on for a few days. We thought, *Okay, so she wets the bed.* A lot of four-year-olds suddenly start to wet the bed, especially when there's some upheaval, like a move clear across the country to a new city. We'd just pulled Frannie and her sister from everything they knew, so it made sense she was a little out of sorts. We thought, *Okay, so she's crabby.* A lot of four-year-olds are crabby. She'd always been kind of a pistol, anyway, and we'd just started her at a new school. There were so many changes going on that we thought it was all tied in.

Finally, we ran out of reasonable explanations to justify Frannie's behavior, but by this point we had a hunch. Lino researched diabetes on the Internet, and we grew worried enough to call our daughters' pediatrician in Denver, to get her take on what was going on. Looking back, I think it was the bed-wetting that finally pushed us to do something. It was going on for too long for us not to be concerned.

Our pediatrician, Jody Mathie, called us back. When I told her Frannie's symptoms she said, "You need to take her in right now." I asked if we could just bring her in the next time we came home to Colorado, but Dr. Jody said, "No, you have to take her in now."

We got the name of a local pediatrician and made the earliest available appointment. On some level Lino and I both knew what Frannie was facing, because he took off from work and met me at the doctor's office. In a two-career household, that's a sure sign that a situation is serious, because it sometimes seems it takes an act of God, or at the very least a school recital, to get *both* parents to show up during the work day at the same time.

All that's required to diagnose Type 1 diabetes is a simple finger prick and a urine test. Within minutes we were driving frantically to Georgetown University Hospital, and Frannie was being admitted. We hardly had time to think what was happening. My heart broke for Frannie—for *us*—but there was no time to grieve. We had a sick daughter to care for.

A doctor came by to tell us Frannie would need insulin injections for the rest of her life. She would have to be monitored constantly. Every time she ate. Every time she exercised. Every time she went to bed. I suppose I already knew this, but to have it laid out for me in plain, clinical terms in relation to my own little girl was devastating and terrifying. I couldn't see how we'd get through it, but at the same time I thought, *Of course we'll get through it. That's just what you do.*

Then another doctor came by who said if our four-year-old daughter had to have a life-threatening disease, Type 1 diabetes wasn't such a bad assignment, because we could learn to manage it. Plus, diabetes was one of the diseases for which medical researchers were discovering exciting avenues toward a cure. This second doctor actually said there was reason to expect a cure in Frannie's lifetime. I found it comforting to think that some of the best scientists in the country would be working on this, for Frannie.

Underneath that hope and comfort, I also found the consultation a little odd, because naturally I disputed this doctor's assertion that my four-year-old daughter had to have a life-threatening disease. No, I thought. She doesn't. But then I understood his point. Even Frannie, at four, could learn to manage it, this philosophical doctor said.

Our first challenge, of course, was to explain to a four-year-old that the rest of her life would involve blood tests and shots. Dr. Douglas Sobel at Georgetown painstakingly explained diabetes to Francesca, who up until then had no idea she even had a pancreas, much less that it no longer contained the islet cells her body needed to process the sugar her cells required to stay alive.

"You will need to take a special medicine three times a day," Dr. Sobel patiently said.

"What does it taste like?" Frannie quite reasonably wanted to know, fearing forced spoonfuls of yucky-tasting goop like the syrupy red cough medicine she detested.

I winced.

"You don't taste it," Dr. Sobel said, trying to be reassuring. "You take it in a shot."

This, apparently, was a far more terrifying prospect than a daily dose of yucky-tasting goop. Frannie's face turned white. She was uncharacteristically speechless.

One of the first things you have to learn as the parent of a diabetic child is how to administer the finger pricks and injections. The nurses tell you that you can't leave the hospital until you can do it. It's a trial-by-fire sort of deal. They had us practice on an orange; when we felt we were ready, we had to do it to Frannie.

They really threw us right into it. It was the most difficult, dispiriting thing. I was a great big coward about it at first. I had a tough time piercing the skin of the orange, and an even tougher time imagining that this was what our life had now become, all on the back of this sudden diagnosis. I've since spoken to a lot of parents who said they tried the needle on themselves before trying it out on their children. I thought of that, but I worried that once I gave myself a shot I could never muster the courage to inject my little girl. That would have just been too much. Lino always joked that he had not pursued a medical career because of his squeamishness at the sight of blood, but even he managed to do whatever it took to care for Frannie.

We figured the best course was to plow ahead, so I found the strength from a nurse who showed us how to administer the injection and gave Frannie her shot. Anyway, I tried. She saw me approach her with the syringe and crawled underneath the hospital bed, grabbed onto the frame, and wouldn't come out. I had to crawl right under there with her, and it was a good long while before I could get her to leave the comfort of her tiny safe space beneath the mattress springs and to sit still.

It was an awful, agonizing moment for all of us—but we got through it, somehow. And it wasn't so difficult after that. We got through everything that came next, too: the diet, the monitoring, the medications. You find room in your life and in your head for complications you never thought you could handle. You learn what forty-five grams of carbohydrates look like for breakfast. You learn how to search for foods with no carbohydrates. You learn where to look online for answers to the scary questions that invariably surface in the middle of the night, and you learn when to call your doctor immediately and when to put off that call until office hours resume the next morning. You learn to call ahead when you're traveling and learn the locations of the nearest hospitals and emergency treatment centers. You learn how to administer three shots of insulin each day without even thinking about it, and how to do four or five finger-prick blood tests each day, as well. You learn about blood sugar levels and convulsions and all kinds of things you thought you'd only have to watch on *ER*. And then there are the new developments or advances in technology. They are supposed to make your situation easier—but at first, they only seem to complicate it. You learn about those, too.

The disease becomes your life—that is, until you get so familiar with it that you're able to get to where you don't even think about the diabetes anymore, because it's become a part of you and your family. You adapt to it until it's fully absorbed. In our case, we did not want to become one of those families whose lives centered on diabetes. Frannie—and the rest of us—would learn the diabetes regimen, but we did not want her to be known among her peers or her school community as "the diabetic." It would be a part of her life, but we would not let it become her entire life.

Of course, Lino and I didn't think about any of this when Frannie was first diagnosed. All we knew was that we were overwhelmed and looking down a long, difficult road. Quite honestly, I had no idea how we'd manage—how I could be there for Frannie and at the same time do my job. For a while, I thought seriously about leaving Congress. It was too much for me and my family to deal with, all at once. And it didn't *feel* right to be pulled from Frannie at a time like this. It was the diabetes that was pulling at us and changing things up on us, and at the same time it was my relatively new job in Congress.

But there was nothing I could do about the diabetes. It was a fact of our life. There was, however, something I could do about my career. It was my reality, but it was a changeable reality. I wondered how I could balance caring for a child with a terrible disease while I was logging these long, ridiculous hours on Capitol Hill, getting into long, ridiculous debates on practical, common-sense initiatives that were somehow regarded in this conservative political environment as subversive.

On the other side of the argument was the comforting thought that at least I was with Lino, Raphie, and Frannie during the week, in the early mornings and evenings, which was the time I was most needed at home.

And keep in mind, it wasn't just Frannie and her illness that stood as my distraction. There was also her big sister, Raphaela, who was getting the short end of things at home. In just a brief time, our entire household became centered on Frannie, so we had to try to find a way to let Raphie know we loved her, too. And so, yes, there was a lot on my mind. More than I'd counted on, that's for sure. I also had my constituents to think about. The good people of Denver had just sent me to Washington to represent their best interests. It had hardly been a year, and here I was worrying I didn't have it in me to do the thorough job my position demanded, the job my constituents were used to and fully deserved.

I looked ahead at my voting schedule, my committee hearings, the constituent-service work that's a big part of a representative's day-to-day job, and then on top of that I looked at Frannie and her doctor's appointments and staying on top of her diet and medications. All these things took time and energy. I didn't think I had nearly enough of either to go around, but somehow I found reserves I didn't even know I had. For a while, there seemed to be enough left over for me to take care of my family and the voters in my district back home.

Somewhere along the way, within the first week or so follow-ing Frannie's diagnosis, I realized it might be logistically possible for me to take care of Frannie and attend to my family's needs at home, and at the same time be an effective member of Congress—although I still didn't think it was practical. Sure, it was do-able, but did I really want to log all those hours away from home, away from my daughters, at a time when they needed me the most? I went from leaning one way, thinking I'd have to quit, to leaning the other, thinking I could keep working, to thinking I had no business even having this argument with myself in the first place. Really, it made no sense for me to keep working. I couldn't justify it.

And then, I realized that as a member of Congress I could have a far greater impact on finding a cure for diabetes than I could as a concerned mom. I also realized that our family could turn our new awareness into action and hope, rather than just turning Frannie into the victim of a terrible disease. I wasn't ready to give up my seat in Congress just yet, and so I started to look at my office in a different way. I thought of some great friends of ours back home in Denver—Pat and Andy Loewi, who had adopted a child named Sammie who turned out to have muscular dystrophy. Raphie and Sammie were in the same toddler play group at the time Sammie was diagnosed. The disease quickly became a calling for Pat and Andy. They started raising tens of thousands of dollars each year for muscular dystrophy research. Pat and Andy took what could have been a terrible family tragedy and made it into a family crusade. They never saw themselves or their daughter as victims, and they had a real impact on helping researchers seek a cure for their daughter.

Sadly, this past year, we lost Andy too young to cancer, but Sammie remains a courageous young woman—now a smart and talented high school senior. And her family is continuing its commitment to curing muscular dystrophy. Each year, when I receive an appeal from the Loewis, announcing their annual fundraiser for the Muscular Dystrophy Association and discussing the latest scientific breakthroughs, I think, *Good for them, turning a negative into that kind of positive.*

And now here I was—here *we* were—going through some of these same emotions with Frannie. It occurred to me that I was uniquely positioned to do something more than raise money. From my perch on the Health Subcommittee in Energy and Commerce, I could help draft legislation that might make it easier for scientists to solve the medical puzzles of our time. Already, there was talk about exciting breakthroughs in the area of embryonic stem cell research, with potentially positive implications for patients suffering from Alzheimer's, Parkinson's, stroke, diabetes, and other diseases. I kept coming back to this line of thinking. I could get appropriations and direct millions of dollars to research. I could help raise awareness in the fight against diabetes. I could do all kinds of things, to turn our different kind of negative into a different kind of positive, and in this way help not only Frannie but thousands of little children just like her. I could help create an environment filled with hope, which I now knew from firsthand experience was the one thing parents of sick children had in terribly short supply.

So I stayed on. We made a family decision; it fell to Lino to do a lot of the heavy lifting at home, and he was up to it. He was working full-time, but in his free moments he learned how to count carbs, give Frannie her shots, and test her blood. Over time, he got really good at that and became better than I could ever have been at monitoring and adjusting her blood sugars. He also got really good at combing out the knots in our daughters' hair and helping with homework and taking them on field trips to museums and other attractions in Washington on the weekends when I went to Denver to work.

That's my husband for you, always with the program.

Raphaela stepped up to the plate, too. At age ten, she learned to administer her sister's blood tests and count her carbohydrates and give injections—all of which might explain why she announced at a very young age that she wanted to be a doctor. She's now an undergraduate at Brown University, studying biology and public health.

As it happened, we made a good go of it for a while in Washington, but about five years after I was first elected to Congress, we moved the family back to Denver year-round. Once again, it was a family decision. I stayed on in Congress, but we were going broke and running ourselves ragged trying to maintain two households. We had our house in Maryland and our real home in Denver. I would go home to Colorado every other weekend, and during the Christmas break and in the summers we would move the whole operation back to Denver, while Lino worked out of his firm's Denver office and I would reverse the commute. It was just too much. We looked up one day and realized we were never really in the same place at the same time, all four of us under one roof. I never could find the right shoes, or the right outfit, or the position paper I thought was resting on my nightstand that I meant to read before turning in.

Here's just a taste of how crazy things were for us back then. Gary, our house sitter, called me at my office one day with the bulletin that a squirrel had scampered down the chimney and into our Denver living room and was presently trying to chew its way through the frame of the doorway leading from our dining room to the backyard. He asked me what to do. I told my staff to hold all calls; something had come up. From my desk in Washington, I managed to find the name and number of a critter removal service in the Denver Yellow Pages and arranged to have the squirrel relocated to the great outdoors.

At the same time, we were combating an infestation of giant hopping crickets in the basement of our home in Maryland. Worrying about one set of animal invasions was bad enough, and Lino and I took this squirrel break-in as a sign that we should probably simplify our lives and settle in one house or another.

We started to weigh some of the pros and cons of returning to Denver. On the plus side, Denver happened to have one of the two best diabetes centers in the country. One of them is the Joslin Center in Boston, and the other is the Barbara Davis Center for Childhood Diabetes in Denver. It was established by Marvin Davis, the oil magnate who at one time owned 20th Century Fox, the Oakland Raiders football team, and the Aspen Skiing Company. He founded the center after one of his daughters was diagnosed with diabetes. People actually move to Denver because of this wonderful facility, so that was a big plus on our list of reasons to move back home.

The big negative, of course, was that I didn't want to be separated from my family—not even for a series of short stretches. But ultimately Denver won out. It made too much sense for us to head back home, so that's what we did. I rented a room from my classmate Darlene Hooley (D-Oregon), in her two-bedroom condo, and stayed there during the week. Frannie started to visit Dr. Georgeanna Klingensmith—a skilled endocrinologist at the Barbara Davis Center with a reassuring bedside manner—and very quickly became one of the center's star patients. She's really doing great. She's fourteen now and dealing with her illness has become an accepted part of her daily routine, just as everyone told us it would.

There have been some frightening moments, like the time we were at a bipartisan Congressional retreat in Hershey, Pennsylvania. This took place at a time when the Democrats were still smarting from losing their decades of congressional control, and the mood that weekend was tense and strange. The idea for the retreat was for all of us to sit around and talk about our feelings—in a bipartisan sort of way, of course—but my head was focused on keeping Frannie away from all that chocolate.

In Hershey, this can be easier said than done. They've got chocolate everywhere. Even the air in town carries the distinct scent of cocoa from the Hershey plant. Lino and I ran around trying to collect as much chocolate as we could before Frannie had a chance to grab it, but we couldn't get it all. At the time, Frannie was required to eat a fixed number of carbohydrates to maintain a healthy blood sugar level: no more, no less. But of course she succumbed to temptation before long and filled her carbohydrate quota with chocolate, despite our repeated warnings. In all fairness to Frannie, we'd put her in a tough spot. It's difficult to distract a little kid from the evil chocolate when it's piled in bowls in every room in town. At first, it appeared her maturity and willpower would see her through, but after a while she saw herself as a female Charlie, set loose in Willy Wonka's wonderful world.

She ended up stuffing herself with simple sugars, which rapidly increased and then dropped her blood sugar level so that her glucose level plummeted in the middle of the night. I had been worried about her, so I climbed into the double bed in the hotel room next to her. In the middle of the night, she started twitching and shaking uncontrollably. I tried to wake her up, but she was unresponsive. This is all part of a child's reaction to dangerously low blood sugar. Lino called the hotel operator while I tried to figure out how to save my daughter's life. We were plainly terrified.

Within minutes, an ambulance rushed us to the Hershey Medical Center. Frannie was administered glucose to raise her blood sugar. By morning, she was sleeping comfortably—but we were drained. Over the next few years, Frannie had several more late-night seizures. We learned to force her to drink orange juice or ingest cake frosting gel, and if she was unresponsive, we called 911.

These days, though, Frannie's got it under control. She's like any other teenager. She can sleep over at a friend's house. She can play sports. She goes away to camp every summer and attends all the field trips with her classmates at school. She can get on my nerves, being fourteen. Frannie's been on an insulin pump since she was ten, and that's really helped even out her blood sugars. It allows her to eat anything she wants, whenever she wants. She's able to input the number of carbohydrates she's eaten into the pump, which administers the correct amount of insulin. The first day she got the pump she had us take her for a Jamba Juice shake and a cinnamon roll. I don't think she ate for two days after that, but she didn't care. She was able to eat like a regular kid, at long last, and she was happy. She hasn't had a seizure since. Her friends even think the pump is kind of cool—and it is. She's decorated it with a jellybean "skin," like the kids use for their iPods and cell phones. With the pump and the continuous glucose monitor she's used since late 2007, to measure her blood glucose every five minutes, she describes herself as the "bionic woman."

Our decision early on to not let Frannie feel like a victim and to not let our lives be held hostage by this disease was clearly the right way to go. Happily, Frannie appears to have embraced the same attitude. In fact, she came up to me one day and said, "Mom, I hate it when people say I suffer from diabetes. It really irritates me."

I said, "Why is that?"

She said, "Because I'm not suffering at all."

I smiled and said, "No, you're definitely not."

Now that Frannie's fairly thriving, I've found my own political path. Not long after Frannie's diagnosis, a friend of mine on Energy and Commerce, Elizabeth Furse (D-Oregon), decided to retire from Congress and to pass me a key baton. Some years earlier, Elizabeth had founded the Congressional Diabetes Caucus with George Nethercutt (R-Washington). Both of them had grown daughters with diabetes. Elizabeth knew about Frannie, and she knew about my interest in cutting-edge scientific research, so she asked if I would sign on as the new co-chair when she stepped down.

Of course, I agreed. I had already carved out a niche for myself on children's health care issues, so this was a natural fit for me. When I took that position on the Diabetes Caucus it wasn't *just* about Frannie, because my interests in this area pre-dated her diagnosis. But now that we were struggling with some of these same issues at home it became *especially* about Frannie.

No, my abiding interest in children's health care and pioneering scientific research didn't come from a personal place in my life, but it landed there. It hit me where I lived and resonated there. And now I sit and marvel at the great strides my daughter has made, at the healthy and positive way she approaches her life. I see and feel what she has been made to shoulder, and I shoulder it with her, in what ways I can. That's why it angers me to think of George W. Bush sitting up there in the White House, deciding that the welfare of a bunch of frozen embryonic cells is somehow more important than the welfare of my child—or the welfare of any child for that matter. There are thousands and thousands of parents just like me, whose kids have diabetes or cancer or muscular dystrophy, who feel the same way; and, there are thousands and thousands of adult children whose parents have Alzheimer's or Parkinson's or stroke. Together we're counting on those embryos to see us through and take some of that weight off our shoulders and set our world right once again.

Our thinking is, if science has taken us to the precipice of these kinds of discoveries, where cures or solutions to all kinds of medical puzzles are suddenly within reach, then we ought to create an environment where scientists can pursue this research in an ethical way, with federal funding and a clear conscience. Anything less, to me, is unacceptable.

My daughter Frannie taught me that.

SIX

ANGELS DANCING ON
THE HEAD OF A PIN

When I became co-chair of the Congressional Diabetes Caucus in 1999, it opened an important door into areas of scientific research filled with hope and possibility. It was through my work with the caucus that I learned more about an exciting advance that could potentially lead to the cure of Type 1 diabetes.

A little background: Scientists believe that Type 1 (or juvenile) diabetes results from an auto-immune response that causes the body to destroy all of the insulin-producing cells in the pancreas. These cells are known as *islet cells*. Once I joined the caucus, I learned that researchers at Harvard and other institutions had been able to use mouse embryos to create what they called *pluripotent cells*—meaning cells that could be scientifically engineered to become any other cell in the body, like these all-important, insulin-producing islet cells. These cells are known as *embryonic stem cells*, and they represented an enormous breakthrough for diabetes patients and their families, but they also held great promise in the area of nerve regeneration from paralysis and in the treatment of Parkinson's, Alzheimer's, macular degeneration, and other diseases.

However, the advance came with a potential red flag, at least as far as religious conservatives were concerned, and very quickly a controversy surfaced in the swirl of excitement over the nascent science of embryonic stem cell research. At issue were the loaded questions of how and under what circumstances human embryos could be used to produce these pluripotent cells, and whether scientists should be allowed to continue along the path that might help them to find out.

Embryos are a cluster of cells that are a few days old. While there were no insurmountable ethical issues surrounding the creation of mouse embryos, serious ethical questions existed around the creation of human embryos simply for the sake of scientific research. Even those of us on the side of aggressive science understood this full well. When scientists first contemplated working on human embryos, bioethicists and researchers thought deeply about these questions. In December 1994, as a result of these serious discussions and deliberations, President Clinton issued an executive order setting the outside boundaries for further study and barring federal funding for research that required the creation of human embryos. Bioethicists accepted the Clinton directive as a rational, civilized response to the daunting prospects of this new field.

But the debate continued. Indeed, the Clinton directive so concerned the religious right that in 1995 two conservative Republicans, Jay Dickey (R-Arkansas) and Roger Wicker (R-Mississippi), offered a rider to the Health & Human Services Appropriations bill to try to stop research on human embryos. The amendment, now known by the unfortunate moniker "Dickey/ Wicker," banned the use of federal funds for any experiment that created or destroyed human embryos. The amendment did not, however, specifically restrict the use of embryonic stem cells from cell lines created with private funding. Thus, although Dickey/ Wicker stopped researchers using federal funds from creating the stem cells, scientists were able to get around the restriction by using federal funds only for experiments on cell lines previously created using private money.

Another development factored into the emerging ethical debate over this type of research. At the same time that scientists were discovering the possibilities of embryonic stem cell research, the practice of in vitro fertilization was becoming more and more common. This technique, which has helped thousands of infertile couples have children, involves the uniting of sperm and eggs from the hopeful parents in a petri dish. The resulting cells are then used to create embryos, one or more of which are implanted in the woman's uterus. In most in vitro fertilization procedures, doctors create more embryos than might be needed for successful implantation. In these cases, the unneeded embryos are either frozen for later use by the couple or discarded as medical waste.

For a time, it appeared as if this concurrent development in IVF technology might fit itself neatly into some of the ethical concerns surrounding embryonic stem cell research, as stem cell researchers began working with IVF clinics and couples to encourage the donation of these unneeded embryos for medical research. The thinking was that, since the embryos had been created for the purposes of in vitro fertilization and not medical research, and because they were slated to be thrown away, scientists could ethically conduct research on these cells and remain within the guidelines established by President Clinton's executive order.

Anyway, that was the hope.

In 1998, working under this uncertain scenario, scientists at the University of Wisconsin were able to isolate human embryonic stem cells and grow them into specialized cells—another thrilling discovery that held tremendous promise in the search for possible cures for many degenerative and genetically based diseases. Like the mouse stem cells that had been isolated in the early 1990s, these cells were pluripotent and could be coaxed into replicating any kind of cell in the human body.

The advance was so startling and potentially wide-ranging that the National Institutes of Health requested a legal opinion to determine whether federal funds could be used for research on stem cells derived from unneeded human embryos donated by clients of IVF clinics, given the president's executive order and the Dickey/Wicker amendment.

Researchers were heartened by the opinion issued by Health & Human Services (HHS) General Counsel Harriet Rabb, who concluded that the Dickey/Wicker amendment did not preclude the research, because stem cells did not fit the statutory definition of a human embryo. An embryo was defined in the ban as an organism capable of becoming a human being when implanted in the uterus—and, since stem cells could not grow into a human being under any circumstance, Rabb concluded that the government could indeed fund research using stem cells derived from the embryo by private funds.

As a result of Rabb's opinion, HHS established a set of guidelines in August 2000 that essentially reiterated the standing interpretation of the presidential and legislative bans, allowing federal funding for research on embryonic stem cells as long as those stem cells had not been extracted, derived, or cultivated using federal monies. However, the HHS guidelines failed to substantively address any of the ethical issues relating to research in this area. The guidelines basically said that it was okay for researchers to create original embryonic stem cell lines with private dollars and then to use federal money to conduct research on those lines, but there was a whole lot of room for interpretation and confusion.

Rabb's opinion, while calculated to balance the interests of science with the need for ethical research, created an uproar among the religious right. Those of us in favor of continued research might have expected as much. Several conservative members of Congress voiced strong opposition to these new guidelines and to embryonic stem cell research in particular. They apparently could not grasp the nuances of encouraging research that could potentially cure diseases that affect millions of Americans *and* doing it in an ethical way. They were unable to look past the fact that the research involved human embryos. There was no room for argument, as far as our most conservative legislators were concerned. If embryos were involved, it was plainly wrong. Period. I often wondered whether these politicians also opposed IVF but were afraid to say so for fear of alienating their constituents, many of whom could not have had their babies without this technology.

Adding to the confusion was the general lack of understanding among members of Congress about stem cell research. Let's face it, there aren't a whole lot of scientists in Congress. A great many of us are lawyers, with only a smattering of high school science classes to help us make sense of the particulars of this type of research. Quite a few of my colleagues thought the research was being conducted on aborted fetuses. (To be fair, some stem cell research has been conducted in this manner, although not with federal money.) Others were not very clear on what an embryo was. And still others had no idea how these embryos had been cultivated in the first place.

I slogged through the material with a legislator's eye and a mother's heart. I am no scientist, but it was clear even to a layperson that these breakthroughs put researchers on the cusp of some amazing possibilities. I thought about what these possibilities might mean for Frannie and for millions of other diabetes patients all over the world—not to mention the many millions more who suffered from Parkinson's, spinal cord injuries, and an assortment of other ailments and illnesses. All these individuals stood to have their lives transformed. I thought the research was so important I made it my mission to let members know exactly what the press was talking about. I read as much as I could on the subject. I talked to as many experts as I could find who would give me the time of day. In a short time, I became fairly expert in explaining the basics of stem cell biology to a nonscientist—from my own nonscientific perspective.

Over time, the tone and tenor of the debate over stem cells began to change, as members of Congress became more and more aware of the intricacies of the issue and their constituents became more and more aware as well. After a while, I began to compare this ongoing debate to the image of angels dancing on the head of a pin. We were back and forth and all over the place. Every question answered meant another question asked: How many cells were in an embryo? How many embryos were created for IVF procedures? How many would be used in the future by the couples for whom they were created? How did we know that embryos wouldn't be created specifically for scientific research?

The discussions could be exasperating at times, but I loved them just the same, because they had real implications for public policy. And once again, on a personal level, the debate had real implications for my daughter Frannie. For the first time since Lino and I had weighed whether it was in our family's best interests for me to stay in Congress following Frannie's diagnosis, I believed we were on the brink of a real revolution in the state of the science. And it felt like I was right there on the front lines—

not in the lab, of course, doing the actual research, but working to create an environment in which scientists could do their thing unencumbered by the stasis and confusion that had attached to their efforts.

Meanwhile, the 2000 presidential election loomed in the background, and so the debate moved onto a national stage. The right-to-life groups clamored for a complete ban on embryonic stem cell research, while at the same time the 110 million Americans suffering from diseases who stood to gain from potential applications called for further study. No politician in a competitive district wanted to touch the issue, because the general public still didn't understand it very well. All most folks knew was just enough to be alarmed or excited, depending on their perspective.

The scientists in my acquaintance were not exactly the most political bunch, but they were very concerned about the outcome of the election. They just wanted to do good work and to push the envelope on possibility. They simply couldn't believe that what they viewed as a scientific revolution could be trumped by politics. Indeed, when the Supreme Court stopped the recount in Florida following the 2000 presidential election— tipping the presidency to George W. Bush, with the Republicans holding Congress— leading stem cell researchers and disease advocacy groups such as the Juvenile Diabetes Research Foundation (JDRF) became distressed (with good reason, it turned out) that the new president might ban embryonic stem cell research altogether.

With the election, those of us who supported this important research knew we had to spring into action. I strongly believed that stem cell research should not be treated as a partisan issue, and I knew that in order to get the attention of the Bush White House I would need to have Republican support. I also knew that we had to act quickly, because the religious right was pressuring the new president to ban federal funding for embryonic stem cell research as one of his first actions.

From all those months spent reaching out to legislators on this issue before the election, I knew many Republicans shared my views. Moderate Republicans tended to support the research, but so did conservatives like Orrin Hatch, the senior senator from Utah. And so, almost immediately after George W. Bush's inauguration in January 2001, I recruited Jim Ramstad (R-Minnesota) to help me work across party lines. Together, we drafted a letter to the president to express our concerns.

Jim and I reached out to our fellow members of Congress to join us as signatories to the letter. Here again, I was grateful that I had spent the fall before the election educating members about the importance of allowing embryonic stem cell research to continue. It was time well spent, it appeared. Yes, a lot of our conservative members from our most conservative districts still thought the issue was a political hot potato, but Jim and I managed to get more than two hundred signatures asking the president to preserve the research.

Members of a number of advocacy groups also began trying to convince the White House not to ban the research. One of the most prominent examples of this ad hoc lobbying effort was a behind-the-scenes push from former First Lady Nancy Reagan, who had become an advocate of the research after President Reagan was diagnosed with Alzheimer's. Even newly installed Health & Human Services Secretary Tommy Thompson was quietly working with the president and his advisors to convince them not to ban the research—a fact I did not learn until several years later.

For a couple days after we sent the letter, there was no response. After several weeks, there was no response. For months, nothing. All we heard was speculation that President Bush was planning to ban all research in this area going forward. We had hoped the pressure from outside activists as well as the letter from the members of Congress would force the president to reconsider his position, but we couldn't figure out why he refused to meet with us so we could explain our view, or even to acknowledge that he had received our letter. I'd never been on the receiving end of such a snub in my entire professional life, and here it was coming from the very top. It was disconcerting—and infuriating. After a while, of course, we would all get used to this presidential nonresponse, because over his two terms in office President Bush rarely acknowledged the existence of opinions contrary to his own.

Finally, in early August 2001, we learned that President Bush was going to announce some kind of statement on embryonic stem cell research. Having heard nothing from the administration since we had sent the letter, we naturally assumed the worst. The timing was curious. Congress had just gone into its annual recess and President Bush was already at his ranch in Crawford, Texas. I was at the Copper Mountain ski resort back home in Colorado, scheduled to give a speech to a lawyers' convention. Nobody was in Washington to give a reaction to the president's announcement, and because it was August, when many families were on vacation, the American people weren't paying too much attention. I couldn't help but think that's exactly what the White House wanted.

The press conference was called for August 9 at 7:00 p.m., Mountain Standard Time, which conflicted with the time I was scheduled to give my speech. I told the organizers I would be a little late and set out to find a television. The only set I could find was in an otherwise empty bar near the lawyers' reception, so I sat down by myself and prepared to hear the president's announcement.

I was expecting the worst, but what I heard that night was like nothing I'd imagined. The president started out acknowledging that this was a difficult issue and noted that it had been "debated within the church, with people of different faiths, even many of the same faith coming to different conclusions." I thought, This can't be good. It was a little startling to hear this kind of preamble from our commander in chief, who was supposed to make these kinds of decisions based on science and ethics, not religious convictions. The president then went on to explain that he had given the issue "thought, prayer, and considerable reflection," after which he had decided that these human embryos were indeed a form of human life—and thus, "a sacred gift from our Creator."

Once again, I thought, *This can't be good.* I thought surely the research was about to be halted, but then the president's announcement took a surprising turn. He said that there were approximately sixty embryonic stem cell lines that had already been created and that he would allow federally funded research to continue on these cell lines. I was shocked. We had heard a rumor that the president might come up with such a proposal, but we rejected it out of hand because it would have been such a patently political decision. Our thinking had been that the research would either be allowed to go forward, or that it would be banned. There would be no in-between. After all, how could you say that you are opposed to embryonic stem cell research because you view the embryos as human lives, but then agree that research could continue with cells that had already been created from the destruction of embryos? It was unprincipled. It made no sense. And it had no basis in science. After all, if it's immoral to destroy human embryos in the name of scientific research, then why is it okay to use federal money for research on human embryos that had already been destroyed before a certain date?

Here's why the president's decision was patently political: Let's say scientists in another country *did* discover a cure for diabetes or Parkinson's, working with embryonic stem cells. If the Bush White House had quashed all American research in this area, the president would look callous and shortsighted. He would stand for all time as an obstacle to progress. However, if the research turned out to yield a real and fundamental break-through, he could point to this backhanded endorsement of the research that was already underway before he took office and take credit for being a visionary, unwilling to bend on this one issue to the religious right he had helped to fortify. Clearly, this was not a scientific decision. It was a political decision, make no mistake. It was a way for the administration to play on both sides of the fence. That's what was so aggravating about this executive order. It simply took the issue off the political table and left people to think, *Okay, good, a decision's been made. At least we don't have to worry about* that *anymore.* But in the wake of that order there was no political will to do anything, on either side of the argument, because the president had walked such a political fine line.

And there was another problem, as we would soon discover. The legal minds at the National Institutes of Health (NIH) interpreted the president's order to mean that scientists could no longer conduct research on nonapproved stem cell lines in labo-ratories that had received *any* federal money for their facilities or equipment—even if those monies had not been directly ear-marked for stem cell study. As far as science and progress were concerned, it was an unfortunate analysis. What it meant was that if labs wanted to use *private* money to fund embryonic stem cell research, they would have to build completely new facilities, at a cost of hundreds of millions of dollars, because surely some federal dollars would have been used somewhere along the line to support their existing facilities.

This one legal interpretation, flowing from this one half-baked executive order, effectively killed most publicly funded embryonic stem cell research in the United States from that point forward. And then things went from bad to worse. The executive order and the NIH interpretation of that order combined to have a chilling effect on all research in this area—not just in the United States, but abroad as well. It had a real domino effect. Americans should take great pride that the NIH is the largest source of funds for basic research in the world, and that U.S. scientists collaborate freely with their international colleagues in every area of science. Now, though, the president's restrictions inhibited this type of partnership. Our scientists could not contribute to this cutting-edge research because they could not use any cells derived from post-August 2001 embryos. This left scientists in Great Britain, Israel, Singapore, Korea, and many other countries without the critical data and advice they needed to fully utilize their own labs and work to find cures for these diseases.

And so there we were, stuck on the wrong side of progress.

At first, members of Congress on both sides of the aisle were relieved to hear of the president's executive order. They could now move about their business without having to get into the sticky middle of the debate. Most thought naively that research could continue on the sixty-plus cell lines the president had identified, and following the September 11 terrorist attacks on the

United States a month later, we turned our attention to other, more pressing issues.

But I refused to let the matter rest with the president's directive. I kept talking to scientists about the long-term effects of these new restrictions. As it turned out, there were nowhere near the sixty-plus cell lines available for continued research. The way the White House had arrived at that number, apparently, was to call up researchers around the world and ask them how many cell lines they had. Some clinics overestimated their lines; some of the lines turned out to be of a poor quality for research; and some just didn't exist in the first place. In the end, scientists identified fewer than twenty research-quality lines available to U.S. scientists. This was a huge problem. You have to remember, embryonic stem cell research was still in its infancy back then. Nobody really knew if there'd be enough genetic diversity in these few existing lines to accommodate any viable research, just as nobody really knew the quantity or quality of those lines. And all of the lines had been grown using mouse proteins, which meant that there could never be any clinical use for them, since the cells included biological matter that was not from humans.

It was like taking a kid into an abandoned candy store and telling her she could have anything she liked. As a statement of public policy, it was a textbook example of double-speak: It sounded good, but it didn't accomplish anything positive; even worse, it sent a horribly mixed message; and worse still, in purely scientific terms, it set us back.

The more I talked to scientists and disease advocacy groups, the more I realized we needed to do something to turn the situation back to where it had been before August 2001. We needed to put the promise of these early stem cell discoveries back on the table. We had been so close to so many thrilling breakthroughs that could have helped so many millions of people, and now we couldn't sit silently and have all of these potential gains put on pause simply because of the religious ideology of one group.

The general public seemed to question the president as well. According to one poll, 69 percent of Americans favored lifting the Bush-imposed restrictions, and yet the president stubbornly refused to re-examine his policy. Realize, this wasn't a poll of Democrats or Republicans or Independents. This wasn't a poll of pro-life voters or pro-choice voters. This was a poll that reached across the political and ideological spectrum and came back with the startling conclusion that folks wanted to see what science might turn up on this issue. Whatever the ethical implications of this type of research, people seemed to accept it—and yet, the president still held fast.

Out of frustration with the lack of progress in this area, states had begun to take matters into their own hands. In California, in 2004, some influential parents of diabetic children, including the film producers Jerry and Janet Zucker, and Doug Wick and Lucy Fisher, teamed with an activist named Robert Klein to push a statewide initiative called the California Stem Cell Research and Cures Initiative, authorizing spending of about $300 million a year for ten years on embryonic stem cell research. Many other states followed suit—although few could match the resources of a big state like California.

As I saw it, the problem with relying on individual states to step in where the federal government could not was that you'd get a patchwork of solutions and a lack of consistency and oversight. One hand wouldn't necessarily know what the other was doing, and we'd be unable to effectively govern or monitor the research or to apply any type of ethical standard. This would have only made the confusion and uncertainty over stem cells even more troubling. Despite President Bush's stated concern about the ethics of the research, there were no federal ethics rules or guidelines in place governing research on any of these new cell lines, and so to continue research on a state-by-state basis without ethical parameters would have been irresponsible. Also, not even a state the size of California could approach the most basic funding needed to move the research along on the federal level.

As readers may have noticed by now, when I have the courage of my convictions I don't give up on an issue—and here I had that courage in full force. The mounting evidence that the federal restrictions were all but halting embryonic stem cell research convinced me that I needed to make another go at lifting the restrictions. This time I reached out to another Republican colleague, Mike Castle of Delaware. Mike had been governor of Delaware, and now that he was in the House, he had a great deal of respect among both Republicans *and* Democrats. He had a reputation for passing legislation in a bipartisan way, which I believed was necessary here. Together, we decided to refresh President Bush's memory on our opposition to his executive order and to do whatever we could to jump-start this stalled research.

It was, we believed, the will of the people. It was also our responsibility to uphold the common interests of science and progress over a narrow ideological view.

We started with another letter, but—surprise, surprise—there was no White House response.

Neither one of us wanted to wait around forever for the president to get back to us, so we shifted gears and decided to introduce legislation that would overturn the executive order. We were legislators, after all, so this seemed a sound, inevitable move. Mike and I worked hard to craft a bill that both allowed federal funding for stem cell research and instituted a strong set of ethical guidelines to regulate that research going forward. The bill said that federal funds could be used on any embryonic stem cell lines as long as the embryos had been created for IVF, were slated to be destroyed as medical waste, and were voluntarily donated by the couples for whom they had been created. Our proposed bill did not allow any embryos to be created for the express purposes of research, and we did not allow donating couples to receive any compensation for the embryos.

We tried to anticipate every possible moral or ethical objection and to address it responsibly, and when we were done we believed our tightly crafted bill might break the stem cell logjam in Washington, since there was now widespread public support for the research. And there was support in both chambers. In addition to our ongoing effort in the House, a number of U.S. senators were interested in promoting stem cell research, including Tom Harkin (D-Iowa), Arlen Specter (R-Pennsylvania), Orrin Hatch (R-Utah), Ted Kennedy (D-Massachusetts), Dianne Feinstein (D-California), and Gordon Smith (R-Oregon). This group became our bipartisan team in the Senate, and they went to work on their end while Mike Castle and I tried to pass the bill in the House.

Our stem cell legislation was referred to Energy and Commerce, but we never had a hearing about the topic in general or about the bill in particular. I kept trying to get Joe Barton, our committee chairman, to hold a hearing, but he was reluctant to do so. Joe, a conservative Republican from Texas, quite reasonably said, "The subject is too inflammatory. We can't control what would happen."

He was right, I suppose. You don't want to hold a hearing on a volatile issue unless you're fairly confident you can keep a tight rein on the proceedings. With something as heated as embryonic stem cell research, it could have been a real circus.

Ultimately, Mike and I decided not to force the bill to a vote until after the 2004 election because we did not want Republicans to vote against the bill simply because they were trying to support and protect their president in his bid for re-election. We figured that, by waiting, a good number of our Republican colleagues might vote their conscience on this issue instead of voting their party line.

After the election, we wrote the president another letter. This time, we weren't too surprised when we didn't hear back, so we reintroduced the bill in February 2005 and set about trying to bring it up for a vote.

In the U.S. House of Representatives, the leadership is not required to schedule any bill for a vote, either in committee or on the floor. The Speaker of the House, Dennis Hastert (R-Illinois) and Majority Leader Tom DeLay (R-Texas), both stoutly anti–stem cell and closely aligned with the religious right, seemed disinclined to schedule the bill for a vote, so Mike and I tried to drum up support in what ways we could.

Our methods? Well, we mainly used not-so-loaded threats and not-so-gentle persuasion, and by the time we were through we'd tilted heavily in the threat direction.

Mike Castle was a leader of the Tuesday Group, a loose-knit collection of about twenty-five moderate Republicans that met for lunch every Tuesday to discuss issues and strategy. The Tuesday Group considered our bill and decided to make it their top priority in the 2005 legislative session. Mike and the other group members approached the Republican leadership and told them that unless the stem cell bill was brought up on the floor, these twenty-five or so moderate Republicans would vote against key pieces of legislation, including the appropriations bills. This was a problem for the leadership, of course, because the Republican majority in Congress was so thin they needed every vote to pass their agenda.

In the meantime, I did some threat assessment of my own. I went back to Chairman Barton and asked him to support me in my effort to take the bill directly to the floor, bypassing consideration in Energy and Commerce. The committee calendar offered up a convenient power play, which I used to full advantage. We were just getting ready to consider a bill giving prescription drug coverage to senior citizens on Medicare, so I told Joe that if I had to I would introduce my stem cell bill as an amendment to the Medicare bill. I also told him that I had the votes to pass it. Naturally, Joe didn't want to clutter up his bill with a controversial expansion of stem cell research, so he promised to work with the House leadership to bring our bill directly to the floor.

A telling footnote: I didn't know it at the time, but Joe's wife had been the director of the one of the county offices in Texas of the American Diabetes Association, and it turned out he was secretly supportive of my efforts. Of course, I had no idea where he stood on the legislation but assumed because of his self-described "100 percent pro-life voting record" that he opposed the bill, which was why I pushed him so hard on his Medicare bill. Sometimes, assumptions based on party labels can be deceiving.

Mike Castle and I decided that if we were going up against the Republican leadership on a floor vote, we'd better have a hard count of members' positions going in. We were also concerned that members would not know exactly what embryonic stem cell research was, and we were afraid they would be confused by the lies of our opponents. So we started a bipartisan stem cell whip team.

We knew most members' positions on choice issues. When we whipped those issues, we pretty much went to members the advocacy groups had identified as either for us or on the fence. But with stem cell issues, we learned, we couldn't be sure of anyone. There had never been a vote on the subject, so we had to go individually to each member and start from scratch. In some cases, that meant explaining what embryos were, what the research was, and what we were trying to achieve with our legislation. Our bipartisan whip team was a diverse group of intelligent, hard-working, persuasive people who knew how to get a hard vote count. On the Democratic side, I recruited Tammy Baldwin (D-Wisconsin), Lois Capps (D-California), Russ Carnahan (D-Missouri), and Jim Langevin (D-Rhode Island). On the Republican side, Mike recruited Mary Bono (R-California), Jeb Bradley (R-New Hampshire), Charlie Dent (R-Pennsylvania), Fred Upton (R-Michigan), Mark Kirk (R-Illinois), and Joe Schwarz (R-Michigan).

The first few whip meetings were a little tense. A Republican would come in and see Democrats sitting there and say, "Are any other Republicans coming?" The same thing happened when Democratic members met with us. Soon, though, members were exchanging ideas and names just like they'd been working together all their lives. When we got a firm *yes*, everyone on our whip team would get a satisfied look on their faces. If we got a *no* or a *leaning no,* someone would say, "Let me try to talk him into it," or, "What information do you think we need to get to her in order to change her mind?"

Our bipartisan whip effort was not only effective in helping us pass our bill, but it also led to lasting friendships and legislative partnerships. To this day, I consult with several of the Republican members on legislation or on votes, and I know the other members do the same.

As floor consideration of the bill approached, our whip effort intensified. Soon, we were having at least one meeting a day and talking much more often than that. It became apparent that we would have the votes on the House floor to pass the bill (a minor miracle!), but we weren't sure of the totals. At that point, we thought it might make a difference to the president whether we passed the bill by one vote or by twenty votes, so we were unrelenting.

Our stem cell bill was finally scheduled for floor consideration on May 24, 2005—but of course our work on the bill was far from done. We set up a makeshift "war room" in a conference room in one of the House office buildings and brought in researchers from around the country to answer any questions members of Congress might have about the issue. We put on a real full-court press. The researchers came to us through an advocacy group called CAMR—the Coalition for the Advancement of Medical Research—but they might as well have been from Central Casting. Not only did these guys know their stuff, but just as important, they looked the part. They were distinguished scientists, wearing tweed sports coats with patches on the elbows. They had a hard time understanding the nature of political discourse, though. Here's an example: One of the cable news stations scheduled a segment with two pro-research members and two anti-research members, to debate the merits of the proposed legislation. Each speaker had two minutes to explain his or her position. During my allotted time I tried to keep my arguments short and simple. When I came back to the war room, however, the scientists were just apoplectic about the assertions our opponents had made and wanted to know why I hadn't refuted their arguments point-by-point. If I had done so, of course, I would have shot through my two minutes in no time flat, and made no headway on points that needed making. But that's politics. Sometimes, there's no room in the proceedings to answer every question and counter every argument.

And sometimes there's an unexpected wrinkle, as happened here. When the bill finally came up to the floor, we noticed that the leadership had put up a "companion" piece of legislation alongside it—a bill to establish a registry for human fetal cord blood research.

Another backgrounder: fetal cord blood cells are so-called adult stem cells, which have proven effective in treating a variety of blood-based diseases, including cancers. As of May 2005, though, they had shown no practical promise in treating the many and varied diseases we were talking about on the embryonic stem cell front, including Alzheimer's, diabetes, and nerve regeneration.

The attachment of this companion bill was indicative of the frustrating attacks we had to counter, attacks that had no basis in science. The opponents of our bill kept arguing that adult stem cell research was the same as embryonic stem cell research, which was simply wrong. I had to believe the people making the argument knew it was unfounded, but they kept making it just the same in a blatant attempt to confuse members. Fortunately, in the end, no member of Congress was confused. Some were irate, but no one was confused.

This was a shame, because on its face I had no problem with the cord blood registry bill. I thought it was a good idea, even though it had nothing to do with embryonic stem cell research. That's why I urged my colleagues to support that bill as well as the stem cell bill. This wasn't really a strategy, but I believe it came across as such, and I also believe it caught our conservative opponents off-guard. They had assumed we would automatically oppose the cord blood legislation, but how could I oppose it if it made good sense?

After a relatively civil floor debate, we passed our stem cell bill by a margin of 238–194. We got all the moderate Republicans to side with us, and even some Republicans who were not so moderate. We got most of the Democrats, too, even those who considered themselves pro-life. "What could be more pro-life than working for a cure for a loved one?" asked Jim Langevin, a pro-life Catholic who had suffered a spinal cord injury at age sixteen, giving voice to a welcome point of view.

The cord blood bill also passed, by an overwhelming 431–1 vote.

We were excited about passing our stem cell bill by such a solid margin, but our enthusiasm was quickly sobered by the realization that we were far short of the 290 or so votes we needed to override a presidential veto. Still, we decided to savor the victory and worry about the president later.

We immediately called a press conference to announce the passage of the bill and to send it to the Senate. Mike Castle had the terrific idea to actually gift-wrap the bill and present it to our six Senate sponsors at the press conference, so that's just what we did. It turned out to be a great photo opportunity, and we were assured by our bipartisan group of Senate sponsors that they would take up consideration of the bill right away.

During the press conference, Orrin Hatch and the others spoke very graciously about our extraordinary efforts in getting this bill passed, and quite confidently about its chances in the Senate. There was a feeling among our group that we had finally accomplished something. Underneath that feeling was the hope that maybe we would send a message to the president that he should reconsider his position and work with us to expand this research.

After the press conference, Orrin Hatch walked over to me and said, "Diana, you're my hero."

At that moment, my whole career flashed before my eyes— and alongside it, a question mark. I didn't know if I should be happy that one of the conservative icons of the Senate was telling me I was his hero, or if I should rethink everything. I decided to take is as a compliment, because my whole goal in working on tough issues had been to try to bring coalitions together, irrespective of party affiliation. Finding common ground, that was my thing. Many politicians talk about it, but it is very difficult to achieve in Washington. And here was Orrin Hatch telling *me* I was his hero. It was one of those oddly wonderful political moments, and I took it in and thought, *Maybe we can find some other problems to solve together.*

As it turned out, it took the Senate more than a year to bring up the stem cell bill. (Our sponsors had neglected to tell us that "right away" in the Senate meant at least a year.) In the meantime, Mike Castle and I worked with our Senate allies to try to get the president to meet with us, but he continued to ignore us. It's like he hoped we would all just go away. Still, we believed it would be difficult for the president to ignore the support that was clearly building for this type of research. That support even extended to his own appointees who had once championed the president's executive order of August 2001. Just to offer one example of this shift, NIH Director Elias Zerhouni was asked at a hearing on the NIH budget if the president's restrictions were hampering research. Dr. Zerhouni, who had initially endorsed the Bush ban, admitted that indeed they were.

"From my standpoint," Dr. Zerhouni stated, "it is clear today that American science will be better-served if our scientists have access to those stem cell lines."

We had several bicameral strategy meetings with the senators, and I personally walked across the Capitol to meet with senators, like my friend Richard Lugar (R-Indiana), who were on our whip lists as undecided. (Senator Lugar eventually supported the bill, by the way.) Our thinking was to make double-sure we had the votes to pass the bill in the Senate and to garner enough votes to forestall the presidential veto that seemed to lay ominously in wait.

Finally, on July 18, 2006, the Senate brought up the bill on the floor for a vote. It came up alongside two companion bills: one to ban "fetal farming," the completely abhorrent and as yet unattempted practice of using fetuses to harvest body parts; another to encourage the HHS secretary to fund "alternative" stem cell research, specifically, to "derive human pluripotent stem cell lines using techniques that do not knowingly harm embryos." It was easy to support a bill to ban fetal farming, but at first glance, the alternative research bill seemed like a feeble bill to me; at second glance, even more so. For one thing, the secretary of HHS already had the ability to fund other types of research; only embryonic stem cell research was restricted. For another, funding decisions like this did not need congressional approval. Finally, and most importantly, I saw this bill as a type of fig leaf—an attempt by the anti-research Republican leadership in the Senate to give themselves and the president some kind of perceived cover, a way for them to say they actually supported *something* in the name of science.

Passage of my bill was so momentous, I decided to go over to the Senate chambers for the final vote count.

The first bill considered was the fetal farming bill, which passed unanimously. No surprise there. Next came the "alternative therapies" bill, which to my surprise also passed. As they were beginning to call the roll on my bill, one of the Senate clerks approached me frantically and said, "They need you over in the House right away."

"Why?" I asked.

The clerk said, "I don't know."

It was an unusual summons, to say the least, so I collected my papers and ran across the Capitol, literally. When I got to the House, the fetal farming bill was already being called for debate. Just like that. In all my years in Congress, I'd never seen a bill come to the House from the Senate that quickly. I thought someone must have brought it over on roller skates! The only explanation I could come up with for this haste was that the Republicans wanted to pass these bills quickly, and then get the announcement of the stem cell's bill passage off the front pages of our newspapers as swiftly as possible. Understand, it usually takes three or four days to get a bill to the House from the Senate, and here it happened almost the moment the vote was taken. It was almost unprecedented, but there was a reason for it, as it played out. What I didn't realize at the time was that it wasn't just the congressional leadership looking to pass these three bills with dispatch, but the Bush White House as well. The president had scheduled his veto of our stem cell bill for the very next morning—a not-so-convenient piece of scheduling we were unaware of just yet, but which would become clear soon enough.

Just then, all we knew was that the fetal farming bill was being called up on the floor, so I ran over to the microphone on the Democratic side of the aisle and claimed the time in support of the bill. No one was expecting the two Senate bills to be called up so soon, so none of our key supporters were on the floor. This meant we had some time to fill. I hurriedly told my staff to start rallying the troops and then I started filibustering until they got there.

I said I had no objections to banning fetal farming, just in case some diabolical mad scientist tried to start doing it, but that the issue was really expanding embryonic stem cell research. I then changed the subject and explained in depth what embryonic stem cell research was and talked about all the exciting advances that researchers abroad had made in just the last year, despite the White House restrictions. I talked about the widespread and now mounting public consensus in support of the research and pointed out that the research involved embryos that were slated to be destroyed. I was an old trial lawyer, thank goodness, so I had no trouble filling the time and thinking quickly on my feet until reinforcements finally arrived and we completed the debate.

As we debated the fetal farming bill, we got word that the alternative research bill had now arrived in the House as well. It was called up under the suspension calendar, which meant that debate was limited and the bill had to pass by a two-thirds vote. I was irritated about the attempt to give the opponents a fig leaf to claim that they supported research, and I was also concerned about Congress telling the NIH what kind of research to fund, so I decided to try to kill the bill. This was a daunting task, given that the Senate had just passed the legislation by a vote of 99–0, and no one in the House had seen this bill until it was sent up to us for a vote. There was no debate, and no advance notice.

It's important to note here, there was nothing wrong with the alternative research bill, but even so I saw it as a transparent public relations ploy. It would have accomplished nothing more than to give the Bush White House a supposedly research-friendly out, to cover for its intransigence on embryonic stem cell research. Other than that, it sought to legislate what was already a matter of procedure at federal research institutions like NIH—namely, the aggressive and ethical pursuit of scientific advancement.

I wasn't really sure that I would be successful in killing such an innocuous-sounding bill with no notice or ability to whip, but I wanted to give it a try. I knew, of course, that because the bill needed two-thirds of the votes to pass, I only needed one-third of the votes to kill it. I also knew, however, that the leadership could just bring it back the next day under regular order, where it would surely get the votes to pass. The best I could hope for, really, was to be a thorn in the Republicans' side on this one. At the very least, I wanted to make the leadership sweat a bit and go through some kind of process. Again, little did I know that the president had already scheduled his veto for the very next morning, and that my efforts to upend this frivolous little bill would have a greater impact than I even imagined.

I called Nancy Pelosi and told her I thought we should vote against the alternatives bill on principle. I told her that the bill would probably carry in the long run, since the leadership would likely bring it back the next day under regular order. But I was out to prove a point—and in order to do that, I believed I needed Nancy's support.

She said, "We'll follow your lead."

When my bipartisan whip team came to the floor, I told them we were going to try to kill the bill so our opponents wouldn't have an excuse for voting against our stem cell bill.

And then we set to work. When the members came to the floor, we told them to vote no. Some of them saw no reason to oppose it. Some of them questioned our motives. One member asked, "Why should I vote against this bill? It's stupid, I agree. It accomplishes nothing, I agree. But it doesn't spend money, and it just tells the secretary to do something he already has the power to do."

In response I said, "Congress doesn't want to start dictating which research is funded by NIH, and furthermore we don't want to give our opponents any excuse for opposing embryonic stem cell research."

That was enough to keep the Republicans from the two-thirds vote they needed to carry the suspension vote, and we were able to deny our opponents their little fig leaf—for the time being.

As we debated the two Senate bills on the House floor, we learned that our stem cell bill had passed the Senate 63–37—a solid margin, to be sure. Because the bill had not been changed in the Senate, it went straight to the president's desk. Like the House vote, the result was gratifying, but it was still four votes short of being able to override a presidential veto. Now, all this time later, we were more worried about this shortfall than we had been after House passage, because it had been over a year and the president had still refused to talk to us or budge from his position. What had once seemed a *likely* presidential veto now seemed all but certain. This was especially troubling because in the previous year public support for stem cell research had actually grown. The more people appeared to understand it, the more they appeared to endorse it. One poll put public support at 73 percent, which was a pretty big number on a hot-button issue such as this; even more revealing, my Republican colleagues shared a poll indicating that more than 50 percent of *pro-life* voters supported the research.

Clearly, we had tapped into a national thirst for sound, pioneering scientific research—and it looked from all angles like we had successfully made the case that this type of research could be done in a moral, ethical way that still managed to respect the religious views of *most* Americans.

But our "victory" would be short-lived: the president's veto ceremony had already been scheduled for the very next morning.

SEVEN

SNOWFLAKE BABIES

I went to bed the night we passed the bill expanding stem cell research and defeated the Republicans' alternative research bill thinking there was no way this president could surprise me. I knew full well he would veto our stem cell bill. The only question was *when*. It never occurred to me to consider how.

To be sure, one of the most consistently reliable aspects of the Bush administration has been its inability to shift gears. If a course of action doesn't seem to be working out, our president will stay that course anyway—a stubborn streak that explains a lot, I think.

When I arrived at the office on the morning of July 19, I was still pleased about our double-barreled victory the night before—pleased that our stem cell bill was passed in the Senate and re-passed in the House, and pleased we were able to turn back the fig leaf alternatives bill after the Senate had passed it unanimously. This last was probably only a temporary setback for the right-wing conservatives, I realized, but at that moment I believed we had made an important point and sent a strong message to the White House that our side would not bend to ideology when it came to science.

What I didn't know at the time, of course, was that the president had been counting on passage of that alternatives bill to help bolster the veto ceremony his administration was planning for that afternoon in the East Room of the White House. As the

morning wore on, word got out about the president's announcement, and I finally admitted to myself that the bill Mike Castle
and I had worked so hard to pass would soon stand as George
Bush's very first presidential veto.

That's quite a dubious honor, don't you think? To be the
principal author of the first piece of legislation vetoed by President Bush? Deep into his second term, no less? For a while, I
took great pride in pointing out this little footnote to history,
although I grew tired of the distinction before long. I can't be
sure, but I think it became tiring when the president issued his
second veto for my *second* stem cell bill, as I will relate a bit later
in this chapter.

My staff gathered in my office at two o'clock in the afternoon, and we turned on the television. There was the president,
standing at a podium, preparing to speak his mind on this issue.
But the scene didn't seem right. The president and the setting he
chose made an incongruous picture as we tuned in. I can't stress
enough how *off* the scene appeared at first glance. I had no frame
of reference for it. Typically, you expect to see a cookie-cutter
announcement for this type of veto, with the president standing
at a podium flanked by members of his staff or his administration,
or by senators and members of Congress who stand in support
of whatever is at issue. But as the picture became clear I saw the
president surrounded by people holding toddlers and infants.

I thought, *That's odd*—and it surely was. It was one of those
awkward, *what's-wrong-with-this-picture?* moments. The president seemed uncomfortable and a little bit angry. The children
also looked uncomfortable, and a little bit anxious in what must
have been for them an unfamiliar situation. I looked on and
thought, *Why does the president have all those children with him in*

the shot? Why does he look like he'd rather be just about any place else in the world than in the East Room with all those kids? Most of the toddlers and infants were squirming and fidgeting. One or two started to cry.

I might have laughed, but all I could do was cringe.

The more I thought about it, the more I realized this was probably the worst visual backdrop you could imagine for a White House veto ceremony, and the worst part about it was that it made no apparent sense. The picture became clear soon enough. The children in the background (and in the foreground, and in the president's arms) were known in Christian adoption circles as *snowflake babies*—children born from excess human embryos from IVF procedures that had been donated by genetic parents and "adopted" by parents unable to conceive children of their own.

"These boys and girls are not spare parts," the president intoned, indicating the children in his midst. "They remind us of what is lost when embryos are destroyed in the name of research. They remind us that we all begin our lives as a small collection of cells. And they remind us that in our zeal for new treatments and cures, America must never abandon our fundamental morals."

The children had been flown in with their adoptive parents from all over the country the day before, which explained why our stem cell bill had been on such a fast track for consideration by the House after its Senate passage. They were meant to highlight a frozen embryo adoption program administered by an organization called Nightlight Christian Adoptions. I later learned that this fringe group, along with other similar organizations, actually received federal grants to the tune of over $10 million to support these "adoptions," from the Department of Health & Human

Services under the Bush administration. At the time of the president's veto ceremony, there had been approximately one hundred and thirty snowflake children born as a result of this program—which comes out to almost $77,000 per child. I couldn't count the number of kids assembled around the president, but there were a couple dozen at least, probably about 20 percent of the entire snowflake baby population.

These children are known as snowflake babies, by the way, "because embryos are unique and fragile, just like a snowflake"—according to the Nightlight Christian Adoptions website.

Now, no one on my staff had ever heard of snowflake babies or frozen embryo adoption programs until just this moment. In fact, many people first hear the term *snowflake baby* and think it has something to do with the fact that the embryos had once been frozen. I had also never heard the term *pre-born children* applied to IVF embryos, which these folks seemed to think was a much warmer, much more life-affirming phrase than frozen embryo.

As we learned following the president's veto, there had been about one hundred and thirty unneeded embryos donated to presumably infertile couples by couples undergoing IVF procedures. There are estimated to be over four hundred thousand frozen embryos in fertility clinics in the United States alone. Most of these will be destroyed when they are no longer needed for IVF procedures, which led me to wonder at the president's intent in featuring these snowflake babies at his unusual veto ceremony. If he meant to shine a light on this type of adoption, he must have realized that genetic parents were free under existing law to create an embryo for in vitro fertilization and then to donate it to somebody else. They would have been free to do so under our proposed legislation as well. There was no need for federal funding to facilitate this type of exchange, or to underwrite an organization like Nightlight Christian Adoptions and its stated mission to offer pre-born children a chance to be born. And it was completely unrealistic to think that all of the four hundred thousand frozen embryos would be donated to other couples.

So what, pray tell, was the point of this whole spectacle? Was the White House suggesting the president would like to require all unused embryos to be put up for adoption? Was the president telling would-be parents there was something unethical about IVF and its creation of excess embryos that would not be implanted in a woman's uterus? Or was the Republican leadership simply doing some misguided tugging at America's heartstrings, hoping to get people to think that if it had been up to the soul-less, God-less, heartless members of Congress behind this embryonic stem cell research bill these adorable snowflake babies would never have been born?

The scenario also confirmed for us that the White House had really, really been counting on that alternative research bill to shore up the president's reputation as a friend to science. When that bill was killed, less than twenty-four hours before this East Room ceremony was scheduled to begin, it was too late for the White House to change course. I thought about this and decided that this probably explained why the president looked so angry. We had managed to derail his fig-leaf alternatives bill, and now he had to admit that he was vetoing the embryonic stem cell research bill straight up.

It even appeared that the White House had not had sufficient time to substantively change the president's speech to reflect the unexpected defeat of the alternatives bill, although the president's speechwriters did manage to make some modifications on the fly. "I'm disappointed that Congress failed to pass another bill that would have promoted good research," the president said, midway through his prepared remarks. "It would have authorized additional federal funding for promising new research that could produce cells with the abilities of embryonic cells, but without the destruction of human embryos. This is an important piece of legislation. This bill was unanimously approved by the Senate. It received two hundred and seventy-three votes in the House of Representatives but was blocked by a minority using procedural maneuvers. I'm disappointed that the House failed to authorize funding for this vital and ethical research."

I heard that and wondered if by *procedural maneuvers* the president meant scrambling to vote on a measure that members of Congress had not had a chance to debate or meaningfully consider.

The president then looked over at his new HHS secretary, Mike Leavitt, and instructed him and NIH Director Zerhouni to, "use all the tools at their disposal to aid the search for stem cell techniques that advance promising medical science in an ethical and morally responsible way."

I heard that and thought, *So much for needing* legislation *to explore other types of research.*

Still, I felt a sliver of pride that we had at least stepped on the president's message. We kept him from his picture-perfect ceremony—which, frankly, wouldn't have been so picture-perfect even with the fig leaf bill in hand. And we lived to fight another day.

In keeping with the whirlwind consideration of this legislation and the apparent desperation of the president and congressional leadership to get the stem cell story off the front pages as quickly as possible, we now learned that our stem cell bill was coming back to the House for a veto override vote that very same day. Soon we were back on the House floor, trying to garner the 290 votes it would take to override the veto. We knew this would be a tough job, and that we were much closer to the two-thirds vote we needed in the Senate. However, since it was a House bill, it had to come back to the House first for an override vote. We made all of our arguments again, including the compelling point that there was now a strong public consensus for this type of research, as well as bipartisan support in both chambers of Congress. But the override vote failed 235–193, far short of the margin we needed.

However we looked at it, we were out of options for the moment. Our bill was dead, and there was nothing to do but pull back and regroup. At the very least, we contented ourselves, we had kept the issue of embryonic stem cell research in the forefront. Public opinion had solidified in favor of it. That's why we were able to win so many conservative Republicans over to our side, because their constituents back home had lobbied them to support the measure. And Bush's own NIH director had quite responsibly changed his position—the position the president had used as the basis for his 2001 executive order—and now believed that more stem cell lines needed to be opened up to researchers. In May 2004, Dr. Zerhouni told Congress that making additional stem cell lines available to researchers "may well speed some areas of human embryonic stem cell research." He had claimed that the president's 2001 decision was based on a sound assessment of the research landscape at that moment in time, but that the science had since passed the president by. This was a bold and courageous statement from a member of the administration, and I hoped that Dr. Zerhouni was continuing to work on the president to expand the cell lines available for research. I also hoped he would not lose his job.

In the meantime, though, we had to plot our next legislative move. Not long after the president's veto, I met with Mike Castle and our Senate sponsors and talked about what to do. We knew full well we could build on all of this support going forward. What we didn't know just yet was how we might build on it. Tom Harkin suggested we consider modifying the language of our bill and resubmitting it, to see if the president might seize the opportunity to get out of the corner into which he had painted himself with his hard-line position. This way, he said, we'd give the president and the rest of our opposition something of an out. A number of our senators reported that they were really hearing from their constituents on this, and that the mood of the country seemed to favor aggressive research in this area, so that if we simply tweaked the language it might give some of our reluctant colleagues a reason to vote for the bill the second time around.

I wasn't wild about this idea. As an old litigator, I always made it a point not to negotiate against myself, and I felt our bill was airtight. We had expanded scientists' ability to do research on lines created after 2001 and put all kinds of thoughtful, responsible controls in place. It was a good, strong bill as originally written; it deserved to carry; and I didn't think modifying our language would accomplish anything, especially considering that we had seen no indication from the other side that the president or any of the religious conservatives working against us were willing to negotiate on this issue.

I said, "I don't really know how you would change the bill in any way that would make it more palatable to the president if his objection is in essence a religious one. It's not like we can fool him into thinking it's anything other than what it is."

In the end, I turned my focus to the upcoming 2006 mid-term elections, to see if we could use the stem cell issue to persuade current members to change their minds, and to elect more like-minded legislators, particularly in the House. We didn't need to change the language of our bill, I realized; we needed to change the minds and the make-up of the people who would be voting on it. The way to do this was to start a political action committee (PAC) and attempt to influence a number of these tightly contested races. My campaign fundraisers were enthusiastic about this idea, so we moved it forward. The purpose of my PAC, which I called the Stem Cell Action Fund, was to support candidates who supported ethical stem cell research, as well as other types of progressive research. If I could help even just a few of them get elected, I thought, we might tilt the balance in both Houses, educate voters in each candidate's district, and give ourselves a real shot to fight off another presidential veto.

Very quickly, I learned that others were enthusiastic about the idea as well. My new friends Jerry and Janet Zucker hosted a fundraiser targeting Hollywood donors at their Los Angeles home. Doug Wick and Lucy Fisher helped, and we raised a good amount of money. Next, we raised another important chunk at an event in New York, put together by Louis DuParte. Lino's college classmate Judi Allen and her husband Paul Mulkerrin hosted an event at their home in suburban Denver, which brought in many new donors. And we raised substantial funds on our website, mainly through mailings and at several other events.

Because PACs are usually partisan, designed to elect candidates from one party or the other, people inevitably asked me if I would support a pro–stem cell Republican, and I always said, "Absolutely, if he was running against an anti–stem cell candidate."

It turned out there was such a candidate. His name was Joe Schwarz, a physician from Michigan who was in his first term in Congress. As a freshman member of Congress, Joe had boldly stepped up in favor of my bill, even though he knew it might cost him with voters back home. Still, he thought the research was important and that we had covered most of the ethical concerns in our bill. Now he was being opposed by an anti–stem cell Republican named Tim Walberg, who was running against him in the Republican primary on this very issue.

I offered to donate money to Joe's campaign through the Stem Cell Action Fund, but he turned it down. He said, "I appreciate it, Diana, but I don't think it will help. Plus, I don't need to give my opponent another reason to attack me for being too liberal."

He was probably right. Joe Schwarz lost the primary by a margin I don't think our small contribution would have been enough to fill, but he went down fighting. Later, he considered switching parties and running against Tim Walberg in the general election, but I think he decided the Republican voter registration edge was just too great in his district. I miss working with Joe to this day; brave legislators who are willing to forfeit their seats to do the right thing are few and far between.

I also decided to travel to swing districts where I thought a pro–stem cell candidate had a chance of defeating or replacing an anti–stem cell candidate. The issue was still very much on the minds of the electorate as the fall elections approached. In August 2006, National Public Radio commissioned a survey of swing voters to determine the issues of greatest importance to them. What was the number one issue that might have persuaded voters to switch their support from one congressional candidate to another? Embryonic stem cell research, by more than twenty points. This was more than double the number of any other issue that tallied in the survey, including the economy and the war in Iraq.

The Republican pundits kept telling the press that stem cell research was not an issue for the 2006 elections because when Americans were polled and asked to identify their top three concerns, stem cell research did not rate overall. When reporters called me and asked about this, I suggested that stem cell research was probably not an issue that would spring to voters' minds—unless they or a family member suffered from a disease the research could potentially help—and maintained that it was an issue that would differentiate one candidate from another when voters decided who to support in the election. The NPR poll demonstrated this clearly.

Along the way, I started calling stem cell research our *positive* wedge issue. It wasn't like the traditional wedge issues the right wing always trotted out to push the electorate—issues such as abortion and gay marriage. (Not incidentally, these issues also failed to land in most voters' top three, but were frequently used as powerful persuaders in an election.) Those issues were negative and divisive, and they tended to cut along party lines. Stem cell research was an issue of hope with strong bipartisan support. When a candidate came out against stem cell research, that move tended to marginalize him or her as a member of the far right—no matter how much time they might have spent trying to appear moderate—so it offered a real litmus test in some of the swing districts around the country.

One of our pro–stem cell candidates was Patrick Murphy, who was running in a suburban Philadelphia district against an incumbent Republican who had voted against our bill. Patrick was an Iraqi veteran, but he was also decidedly pro–stem cell, so he ran on the war as well as on progressive scientific research. His campaign put together a series of very effective commercials, featuring a woman suffering from Alzheimer's and calling for ethical stem cell research.

Another candidate was right in my backyard. Ed Perlmutter, with whom I had served in the Colorado legislature, was running to replace Bob Beauprez, a conservative anti–stem cell member who had decided to run for governor of Colorado. Ed was enmeshed in a tough primary in one of the top ten targeted Congressional seats in the country, a suburban Denver district. He ran television ads featuring his daughter Alexis, who is epileptic, also calling for expansion of stem cell research. Ed won the primary and defeated a conservative Republican in the general election who had once been against my legislation but waffled badly.

Both Patrick and Ed insist that one of the major reasons they were elected was their support for my bill—and they were joined in Washington by many other new pro–stem cell members from around the country.

I think that our extra effort on the stem cell issue was one of the principal reasons the Democrats finally took the majority in both houses of Congress that year. The 2006 mid-term elections weren't *just* about stem cells, of course, but candidates' positions on this type of research helped to define a great many campaigns across the country and offered up a true read on the strength of the religious right.

When Nancy Pelosi became the new Speaker of the House, she announced that our stem cell bill would be one of her top six priorities for the coming term—her "Six for '06," she called it. When the new Congress convened, Nancy announced that the bill would be considered as the third bill of the new Democratic agenda, and so it was introduced as HR3. Again, I sponsored the bill with my trusted ally, Mike Castle.

Our Senate sponsors suggested that we start off in the Senate this time, because it seemed like we might now have the numbers for an override, and it was still unlikely that we had sufficient votes in the House. The thought was that we could pass the bill in the Senate and that the overwhelming vote in that body would give us an extra push in the House. It would also put more pressure on the president to at least talk with us before he vetoed the bill again. That sounded like a good strategy, so I asked Tom Harkin when he was planning to bring it up in the Senate.

He said, "Right away."

I said, "Define right away."

He said, "As soon as we can."

Here again, we'd learned the hard lesson that, in the Senate, *as soon as we can* might mean anything from a couple of weeks to late summer, and Nancy decided that we wouldn't wait. We would pass the House bill on the third day of the session and send it to the Senate. That became the plan. The Senate could then either take up the House bill or bring up their own bill and send it back over to the House.

We passed the bill on the third day of the 110th Congress. It was the same bill the president had vetoed the year before. I didn't change the language, because the president and his staff still refused to talk to us. After the fall elections, Mike Castle and I had sent the president another letter, which stated, "Now that there's a new majority in Congress, we hope you'll sit down and talk to us about this issue and see if we can work out some common ground."

We weren't terribly surprised when we got a return letter from the White House secretary, telling us the president was "unavailable."

We looked to our newest members of Congress to help us tilt the scales—an unorthodox approach, to say the least, because according to congressional tradition new members are meant to be seen and not heard, especially during their first few weeks in office. In floor debate on important measures, preference is usually given to senior committee members with jurisdiction over the bill under discussion. But we couldn't afford to let tradition stand in the way of our stem cell battle, and with John Dingell as our newly restored chairman of Energy and Commerce, I encouraged our new members to stand front and center on this issue.

Among the freshman members of Congress who spoke loudly and passionately in favor of stem cell research in general and our bill in particular were Ed Perlmutter, Jason Altmire (D-Pennsylvania), Albio Sires (D-New Jersey), Patrick Murphy, Harry Mitchell (D-Arizona), Zach Space (D-Ohio), Steven Cohen (D-Tennessee), and Joe Sestak (D-Pennsylvania).

In all, we picked up fourteen votes from the 2006 House tally. Dale Kildee, a conservative Democrat from Michigan, had visited with researchers from his district over the Christmas holidays and decided to change his *no* vote to a resounding *yes*. The rest of the shift had primarily to do with the turnover we saw in those swing districts around the country, where sixteen seats switched from anti–stem cell Republicans to pro–stem cell Democrats. We were still short of a veto override, but we were inching closer to that critical two-thirds number.

Next, we sent the bill on to the Senate, but our Senate allies had also introduced their own legislation. Their bill included both the language from our House bill *and* the language from the do-nothing alternatives bill we had killed in the House the previous summer. This was a sound strategy, the Senate sponsors thought.

The idea was that if they included the alternatives bill, which had passed the Senate unanimously the first time around, they might pick up enough votes to override a veto on this second pass.

Nancy Pelosi had been right about the Senate's as-soon-as-we-can timetable. Because of internal wrangling in the Senate, the stem cell vote was pushed to April, so it turned out to be a good move to put the House vote first. The Senate considered the bill with the alternative research language, only this particular gambit didn't work. The bill still passed, but counting the Senators who supported the bill but were absent from the vote, sixty-six Senators voted in favor of our measure—one shy of the magic veto override number of sixty-seven.

The Senate bill was then sent to the House for action. This time, since the Democrats who favored the legislation were in control of the scheduling, we decided to wait for a few weeks to try to put pressure on House members to support the Senate version. At the same time, the anti–stem cell advocacy groups cranked up their efforts to persuade members to oppose the measure, focusing on freshman members and those who had come close to losing their last election to a pro–stem cell candidate. The House scheduled the vote for June 12, 2007, and we pushed the vote to 247–176, still short of the veto override number. We were getting closer and closer each time out, but not yet close enough. Looking back, the inclusion of the alternatives language didn't help us pick up any votes.

Again, since the Democrats were now in control, we could decide when to send the bill to the president. To highlight the issue, Nancy Pelosi and Senate Majority Leader Harry Reid (D-Nevada) scheduled a ceremony to sign the bill in one of the Senate hearing rooms that afternoon. The leadership invited patients who could be helped by embryonic stem cell research to speak and to implore the president to listen to the Congress and the public and expand his executive order, which had now been the law of the land for six years. Then Nancy and Harry signed the joint resolution, sending the bill to the president's desk.

President Bush waited until the end of the week to quietly kill the bill—the second presidential veto on his watch.

There's an adage in Washington (and elsewhere, I suppose) that suggests that if you are determined to take an unpopular action or commit a dastardly deed it's best to do so late on a Friday afternoon, and in this way avoid the press. Relatively few constituents watch the nightly news on Fridays or read newspapers on Saturdays. That's the tactic our president put in play here. There was no veto ceremony, no East Room spectacle, no press conference. There were no snowflake babies. The president just vetoed our bill in the privacy of his office and hoped it would quietly disappear.

Now, at long last, I finally resigned myself to the fact that the president had no intention of ever changing his mind on this issue. It didn't matter what both chambers of Congress wanted. It didn't matter what the public wanted. It didn't matter what the president's own NIH appointee wanted. Regardless of the facts and the scientific advances, he was stubbornly wedded to his position. I realized that if by some miracle there had been a breakthrough by some scientist, somewhere else in the world, President Bush would say, "Well, good for them. At least the discoveries weren't made using *American* embryos." Taking this hypothetical scenario one step further, I imagined that if a cure was indeed discovered using the presidentially decreed immoral stem cell lines—for diabetes, let's say—he would probably try to stop it from being used in this country.

Mercifully, the research does continue, in its own halting way. The state of California passed its own stem cell initiative and is now in the process of establishing its own research centers, after a prolonged court battle. Researchers in Great Britain are close to cures for macular degeneration using human embryonic stem cells. And a researcher in Israel is doing innovative work on nerve cells, hoping to discover a cure for certain types of paralysis.

Scientists in the United States and around the world have also made exciting discoveries with other cell-based research. In October, 2006, just to cite one example, Japanese scientists announced that they had chemically altered mouse skin cells to become pluripotent. In December 2006, scientists at the Medical College of Wisconsin announced the promising development of pluripotent cells from adult hair follicles. And in the spring of 2007, Dr. Robert Lanza of Advanced Cell Technologies in Massachusetts reported that he had successfully removed one cell from an embryo and coaxed it to become a pluripotent cell, claiming that his findings would now eliminate the ethical objections of the religious right because the embryo was not destroyed. Predictably, the religious right rejected Dr. Lanza's assertion— lending a whole new meaning to the analogy of angels dancing on the head of a pin.

In the fall of 2007, scientists working in Japan and Wisconsin revealed that they had succeeded in "programming" adult skin cells to become pluripotent, thus potentially eliminating the need for embryonic stem cells entirely.

Most recently, and perhaps even most significantly, private researchers at the bio-technology company Novacell announced that they had turned human embryonic stem cells into insulin-producing islet cells—one of the first dramatic breakthroughs in embryonic stem cell research in humans. When I learned of the discovery, I couldn't help but wonder (once again) how much farther down the road we'd be with this research if we had been able to use federal dollars to help along the way.

These exhilarating breakthroughs were certainly welcome news to those of us on the side of science, but with each piece of progress religious conservatives attempted to dampen public enthusiasm or to somehow claim credit for holding the line on embryonic stem cell research while researchers pursued the benefits of these other technologies and discoveries.

For the longest time, whenever the president and his Christian conservative allies were asked about stem cells, they leaned back on the same tired arguments. They maintained that federal money should not be used to destroy human embryos, because they claimed it was akin to destroying human life. Forget the fact that a solid majority of Americans supported this research. They trotted out the old lies that adult stem cell research is somehow the same as embryonic stem cell research—whereas in reality the research on the former is at least ten years behind the latter. Indeed, every time there has been a new discovery, the religious right has tried to claim that it, too, was a substitute for embryonic stem cell research.

These days, whenever the president is asked about stem cells in a public forum, he slips into the same sound bite, over and over. If you listen closely, you'll recognize that it's an analogous argument to the line he serves up about abortion, when he says that federal money should not be used for abortions because there is such strong disagreement between pro-life and pro-choice voters. But it's not really the same thing, is it? There's a general public consensus about the ethics of embryonic stem cell research in this country—and it's not like there's a fifty-fifty split, leaning slightly toward stem cells. No, there's a real consensus on this issue, which means that the president's argument has been reduced to the position that federal money should not be used to destroy human embryos because he, George W. Bush, personally disagrees with this type of research. That's the bottom line of it for him—and, unfortunately, for *us*. Does that mean that if just one of my Denver constituents believes strongly that we shouldn't use federal money to continue the war in Iraq that we should stage an immediate pull-out? It's just not a legitimate argument, is it? And yet the president looks to play it both ways. He sanctions the use of federal money to subsidize this ill-conceived snowflake baby/frozen embryo adoption program—a program that could certainly continue without federal money, within existing law—as if every unneeded frozen embryo that results from IVF will be adopted rather than donated for research. And yet the overwhelming majority of Americans support expanding our efforts in embryonic stem cell research.

And so it goes . . .

All of which takes us up to this latest adult skin cell breakthrough. When scientists announced this discovery, the religious right was overcome with excitement—not at the advance itself, but at the perceived opportunity it presented to claim a kind of I-told-you-so victory. The White House even got into the act, insisting that it was the president's restrictions on embryonic stem cell research back in 2001 that forced researchers to head down this new path. And the most troubling piece was that the media bought into this contention. The *Washington Post* even quoted Dr. Lanza comparing his colleagues' discovery to the Wright brothers' pioneering efforts in the field of manned flight.

Whenever I hear that kind of hyperbole, my antennae go up. I'm skeptical, that's my nature. I'm always thinking the Republicans have something up their sleeve—perhaps because they usually do. Following this adult skin cell advance, I called Dr. Larry Goldstein, a respected stem cell researcher now at the University of San Diego, to get his take. Dr. Goldstein told me that, while the new discovery was exciting and promising, it certainly was not the golden bullet substitute for embryonic stem cell research conservatives were making it out to be—or for any other research, for that matter. It turns out that retroviruses were injected into the adult skin cells in order to coax them into becoming pluripotent. Retroviruses can cause genetic changes in the cells, which lead to cancerous tumors, so clearly the research is not yet close to any kind of clinical application.

"In fact," Dr. Goldstein reported, "these retroviruses can be so carcinogenic they are dangerous in a laboratory setting."

Not a substance I would want being used to make islet cells for Frannie, that's for sure.

So what is the answer?

Whenever I talk to people about research, I tell them that it is not the job of government to pick and choose among scientific research methods, so long as the research is legal, ethical, and responsible. I don't believe politicians should point to one method or another and say, "That's the one!" We don't have the information or the expertise—and besides, that's not how the scientific method works. Instead, we should support all ethical cell-based research and see where it takes us. The American people overwhelmingly concur, believing that responsible research using cells taken from donated excess frozen embryos that would otherwise be incinerated as medical waste is ethical.

The recent advances in cell-based research are so exciting I believe we need a Manhattan Project at the National Institute of Health. The same dedication and commitment that led to the development of the atomic bomb could be focused on finding cures that could save millions of lives. We need a greatly enhanced federal budget for research that embraces all ethical techniques, including embryonic stem cell research. And we need strict ethical guidelines to give consistent federal oversight to scientists conducting all of this cutting-edge exploration.

In the meantime, science marches on—and double-speak marches on, too. George W. Bush and the religious right continue to circumvent and undermine these breathtaking discoveries in the name of God and a moral compass that points suspiciously in one direction. Our only hope, I've come to realize, is to march along our own path—and work like hell each November to elect open-minded, thoughtful, curious leaders who just might care enough about the scientific method to make this life-altering research a priority.

EIGHT

SEND IN THE CLONES

"On matters of life and science," President Bush declared during his State of the Union address on January 28, 2008, "we must trust in the innovative spirit of medical researchers and empower them to discover new treatments while respecting moral boundaries."

As the president made these remarks, I was seated in the middle of the House chamber—in the direct sight line of House Speaker Nancy Pelosi, my good friend and trusted ally in the years-long fight for ethical scientific research. This didn't sound to me like the same George W. Bush who had stiff-armed medical researchers for the previous seven years of his presidency, and I knew the words would strike the same false chord with Nancy. Sure enough, when our eyes met across the floor of the U.S. House of Representatives, we flashed each other a shared *are-we-hearing-what-we-think-we're-hearing?* look.

Yes, apparently, we were.

The president continued: ". . . and as we explore promising avenues of research, we must also ensure that all life is treated with the dignity it deserves. And so I call on Congress to pass legislation that bans unethical practices such as the buying, selling, patenting or cloning of human life."

This was almost too much for me to hear from the president's mouth, because since Dolly the sheep was cloned in 1996 members of Congress have been trying to do just as he recommended— to ban reproductive cloning. The president's own party and the religious right have stood in the way, however, because they not only want to ban cloning of humans, also known as *reproductive cloning*, they want to ban legitimate scientific research that uses similar techniques, also known as *therapeutic cloning*.

As the president talked about matters of cell research and science, I could feel the eyes of my colleagues upon me, looking for guidance on whether we should applaud or do nothing in response to his recommendation. I thought, *Well, I imagine he* means *more than he actually just* said, *but I still agree with the actual words.* Of course, almost everyone in Congress agrees we should ban reproductive cloning—and responsible scientists and the majority of Americans concur. And yet it wouldn't do for me to refuse to stand and cheer this comment, while my Republican colleagues all applauded, because then it would look like I thought people should be cloned.

So I stood and applauded, and my colleagues on the Democratic side of the aisle followed suit.

As we stood, the president looked straight into my eyes, and then he smiled. At first I thought I was just reading something into the moment, but I wasn't the only one who had that impression. Several of the people sitting around me noticed the same thing. One of them whispered to me, "He's looking right at you."

I stood there applauding with my House colleagues and considered the president's charge to Congress to pass legislation that bans reproductive cloning. I thought, *Gee, isn't that what we've been* trying *to do?* Then I wondered if this was some sort of game to the president. He probably thought it was funny for him to say something and see if he could get the Democrats to stand and applaud—thus the smile when we stood.

But, of course, the issue of human cloning is not even remotely funny. It's probably the most explosive bioethical issue confronting legislators today. It's also one of the most misunderstood. The concept of cloning, the process of creating an identical copy of one living thing or another, has been around for centuries. But it's only recently, as the concept has become a reality, that bioethicists, medical researchers, Christian conservatives, and, frankly, all the rest of us have become so concerned—even as that concern might be misplaced at times.

Most people know just enough about cloning to raise their own personal red flags—or not quite enough to come to an informed, science-based opinion about it on their own. They know some antique vision of reproductive technology and biological engineering, as imagined in Aldous Huxley's classic 1932 novel, *Brave New World.* They know the slapstick vision, as offered in Woody Allen's 1973 science fiction comedy, *Sleeper.* They know that in 1996, researchers at the Roslin Institute in Scotland successfully bred an exact copy of a six-year-old ewe—the first mammal to be successfully cloned from the cell of an adult animal, a genuine leap that followed the successful cloning of a tadpole in 1952 and a carp in 1963. The "birth" of that one sheep—named Dolly, in honor of Dolly Parton—made headlines all over the world and kick-started the debate on the moral and ethical implications of this exciting breakthrough.

Here in the United States, and around the world, researchers began to consider where this significant discovery might take us. Was it scientifically possible to replicate a human being? And, if so, was it moral? As scientists began to plumb this question, they realized that the cloning of Dolly the sheep was not accomplished without significant trial and error. Scientists cultivated nuclei from sheep cells and sought to transfer them to unfertilized sheep eggs that had been altered to accommodate the engineered nucleus. In this manner, it took 277 eggs for scientists to create twenty-nine embryos, which were then implanted into sheep. One of those resulting pregnancies culminated in the birth of a live lamb—an exact genetic replica of the six-year-old sheep that provided the transferred nucleus.

Early on, it was feared that Dolly would have genetic malformations that would make it more susceptible to diseases and early aging, due to the fact that it was created from a sheep that was already six years old. Those worries were never conclusively confirmed, but the implications of these findings led to widespread agreement among scientists that human reproductive cloning, while theoretically possible, was not ethical. Those conclusions led activists to call for international cloning bans.

More than a decade later, we're still caught in the swirl of that same debate, and much of the discussion has been riddled with confusion. What most people don't know is that there are generally two types of cloning under discussion among bioethicists, lobbyists, activists, and legislators, as mentioned earlier: reproductive cloning and so-called therapeutic cloning, also known as somatic cell nuclear transfer (SCNT), which involves the replication of cells for research purposes only. SCNT has shown similar promise to embryonic stem cell research, although scientists are much further along in their efforts with embryonic stem cells. With SCNT, cells are taken from the body, and the nuclei are replaced. The cells are thus capable of being made into stem cells, which can in turn be programmed to become any type of cell in the body. This type of research dovetails neatly with some of the latest advances in stem cell research, and there is wide agreement in the scientific community that SCNT holds enormous promise for cures and treatments.

The great hope of SCNT is that eventually scientists will be able to take a cell from a patient's body and transform it into an islet cell capable of producing insulin or becoming a nerve cell or another type of cell, filling some other important function for that patient. It's the "spare parts" argument that gets tossed around on both sides of the debate—the far-off idea that scientists might some day be able to create a duplicate liver or kidney to replace a patient's original model. Certainly, the applications for such an advance are astonishing—the stuff of science fiction—but that's where the research could be headed, if it's allowed to continue in an ethical, unfettered way.

Whenever I get deep into the nitty-gritty of SCNT or embryonic stem cell research, I must remind people that I have only a high school biology background. However, in the years since high school I've surrounded myself with some of the brightest, most innovative scientific minds and collected a vast store of accessible research, and I've been able to process some of this valuable information and find a way to explain it so lay folks like me can understand.

Here's the key: Because SCNT researchers can genetically copy a cell drawn directly from a patient's body, that cell will share the patient's DNA. Why is this so important? If scientists simply took an embryonic stem cell capable of performing these necessary functions and placed it into the patient's body, the body would be inclined to reject it, just as it might reject a donated liver or kidney. It's a foreign organ, so you'd have to put the patient on immunosuppressive drugs for the rest of his or her life. For a diabetic, for example, the drugs could have such a profound negative effect that it might negate the positive benefits of the insulin the engineered islet cells might be able to produce. With SCNT, you avoid that problem, so the potential applications and benefits of this type of research are clearly extraordinary.

Reproductive cloning is a whole other issue. This is the process of replicating a human being for no scientific or therapeutic purpose whatsoever. It's replication for the sake of replication— and the dangerous implications of this type of research are immediately and everywhere apparent. It promotes the troubling view that human beings can be designed or manufactured to demonstrate certain characteristics; it blurs the line between nature and science; it ignores the need for genetic diversity in the general population; it opens a dangerous door on the buying and selling of human life; it's unsafe, unproven, and unnecessary.

That said, it is easy to confuse these two different types of research. Since the basic scientific technique is the same, the religious right has decided that both types of cloning should be banned. It would not be difficult to ban reproductive cloning (which nearly everyone agrees should be done) and allow SCNT to continue under closely supervised ethical conditions, but this was where President Bush's insincerity shone through on the night of his State of the Union address. A bipartisan group of us have been trying for years, without success, to get Congress to do just what he asked us to do.

Twice, in 2001 and 2003, Rep. Dave Weldon (R-Florida) introduced legislation to ban both human reproductive cloning and SCNT. Jim Greenwood and I wanted to ban reproductive cloning but preserve important cell-based research, so each time out we offered an amendment to Representative Weldon's bill.

Our amendment said:

It shall be unlawful for any person

(A) to use or attempt to use human somatic cell nuclear transfer technology, or the product of such technology, to initiate a pregnancy or with the intent to initiate a pregnancy; or

(B) to ship, mail, transport, or receive the product of such technology knowing that the product is intended to be used to initiate a pregnancy.

The amendment failed decisively both times, by a vote of 249–178 in 2001, and a vote of 231–174 in 2003.

Boy, we thought. Do we have a lot of education to do with members to let them know the research potential of SCNT! Fortunately, the bill died in the Senate, where there is more support for broad-based research and where Senators Specter and Harkin can stop legislation they disagree with from coming to their committee.

In June 2007, Mike Castle and I introduced a bill to ban human reproductive cloning as a companion bill to our second stem cell bill, so that we could send a clear message that we unequivocally opposed the practice. We decided at that time not to get into the issue of SCNT because we wanted to at least take a step that everyone could agree with. Despite our modest ambitions for the legislation, the House of Representatives defeated the ban, because the National Right to Life Committee believed it did not go far enough because it did not also make SCNT illegal. Indeed, the religious right refuses to support any reproductive cloning ban that does not also ban SCNT—a position that I find unconscionable for the way it confuses a personal system of beliefs with a responsible approach to science. It also makes the weak case that there can be no effective moral or ethical guidelines in the pioneering field of therapeutic cloning that could withstand the unscrupulous and irresponsible behavior we could expect to see from unscrupulous and irresponsible scientists, who would try to clone humans when no one was looking.

I just don't buy that. I believe we have the power to legislate and to regulate our way around these concerns. I believe the marketplace of information and ideas will not tolerate black-market scientists looking to trade on false hopes and an ill-conceived worldview. And, I believe that the most vocal objections to SCNT are voiced in the name of God and not in the name of science—meaning, our elected officials have allowed their personal religious beliefs to get in the way of the public good.

However, I recognize that others disagree with me on this one—rather strongly, in some cases. I respect that. What I don't respect, and can't condone, is that my conservative colleagues have not even allowed us to debate this issue on the facts. The National Right to Life Committee's hysterical response to my legislation shows a complete unwillingness to discuss the issue.

Consider the fairly strident letter of opposition circulated by the committee on the eve of our June vote in the House. The June 5th, 2007, letter began:

> *National Right to Life has received several reports indicating that a bill to foster the creation of cloned human embryos, for the purpose of using them in research that will kill them, will be introduced by Congresswoman DeGette as early as today . . .*
>
> *Such a bill will be falsely labeled as a "ban on human cloning." In reality, it will be a bill to legitimize the use of cloning to create human embryo farms. Under*

such legislation, it will be perfectly acceptable to create, by cloning, any number of human embryos for use in research that will kill them, but it would be unlawful to attempt to allow such a human clone to live by implanting him or her in a womb.

National Right to Life is strongly opposed to this "clone-and-kill" proposal, and will include any roll call on the DeGette bill in its scorecard of key pro-life votes for the 110th Congress . . .

Human embryo farms? Clone-and-kill? How they got that from the bill we put forward is beyond me—and beyond the language in our proposed legislation. I suppose we might have realized that our proposed legislation would be controversial to Christian conservatives, but our bill certainly didn't come anywhere close to the outrageous interpretation of the National Right to Lifers. No, what we meant to accomplish was to ban reproductive cloning and at the same time allow scientists the freedom to pursue SCNT for research purposes—*not* to create or replicate life, and certainly not to destroy it. That's all. It's the very proposal that President Bush put forward in his State of the Union address less than eight months later. But scientific tools like reason and common sense seem to have no place among the pro-life zealots bent on remaking the world in their own ideology.

Nancy Pelosi had decided to place the bill on the suspension calendar because she was certain we could get the two-thirds vote necessary for passage. After all, who could object to a ban on human cloning? But as the overwrought hysteria from the right-to-life community mounted, we realized that we were actually going to lose. The Christian Coalition was willing to tell its allies in Congress to vote against the ban on reproductive cloning in order to make their point about SCNT. And vote against the bill they did: We lost by a vote of 213–204.

I'd love to be in the back of the room when some of my colleagues try to explain why they voted against banning reproductive cloning.

The confusion over cloning has led to some fairly strange hearings on Capitol Hill. One of the most bizarre exchanges I've seen in my political career took place during an Energy and Commerce hearing on cloning. The hearing was held in March 2001, before our Subcommittee on Oversight and Investigations. It was called by Jim Greenwood, who was at that time the Health Subcommittee chairman.

For reasons that have never been made clear, the 2001 hearing included testimony from Dr. Panos Michael Zavos, founder and director of the Andrology Institute of America, who later claimed to have cloned a human being, and representatives of a Canadian-based religious group known as the Raelians. The Raelians are led by a French race-car driver who calls himself Rael. The group, which had approximately 50,000 purported followers, believed the human race was cloned from space travelers 25,000 years ago. They believed this because a four-foot alien reportedly visited Rael atop a volcano and told him as much. At the time of the hearing, the group had received serious attention in mainstream news publications such as the *New York Times*. Rael and his cult-like adherents claimed to have identified an unnamed American couple willing to pay $500,000 to clone their deceased child, although no one could actually produce the couple for confirmation.

It was a classic Washington spectacle—complete with banks of reporters and photographers crouched on the floor, facing the witness table, and waiting for shocking testimony about the first reported cloning of a human being. The Raelians' chief scientist, Brigitte Boisselier, a chemist by training with a specialty in metallurgy, sat next to Dr. Zavos, along with a couple of animal researchers. Rael sat right behind her, appearing as if he had answered a casting call for a cult leader, sporting flowing white robes and a shaved head with a topknot on the crown. Behind him were his acolytes—nubile young women, all wearing tight clothes and matching medallions. Dr. Boisselier, the witness, was herself wearing a see-through blouse. The press was understandably fixated on this strange scene, and the air was thick with the sound of cameras clicking. My colleagues were also transfixed. It was such a weird, surreal moment that I had to remind myself it was actually a congressional hearing and not an outtake from another cloning scene from Woody Allen.

As soon as I had the floor, I went after Dr. Boisselier, to try to discredit her standing. She was easy pickings, I'm afraid. I'll offer highlights of our exchange, culled from the *Congressional Record*, because even all these years later I find it fascinating that an exhibition such as this was allowed to transpire on our public watch:

> **ME:** Now let me ask you what exactly is the research that is being conducted by your organization?
>
> **DR. BOISSELIER:** The first main step that has to be very well done is the enucleation of the egg.
>
> **ME:** And are you, in fact, enucleating the eggs now?
>
> **DR. BOISSELIER:** So they are enucleation of eggs that are performed.

ME: Is that happening now?

DR. BOISSELIER: It's the training of these . . .

ME: Yes or no. Is that happening now?

DR. BOISSELIER: Let me finish. It's actually done on cow eggs.

ME: Okay, so you're doing that with cow eggs now?

DR. BOISSELIER: Right.

ME: What's the second step?

DR. BOISSELIER: Sorry?

ME: What's the second step?

DR. BOISSELIER: The second step is to do the enucleation of human eggs.

ME: And have you done that yet?

DR. BOISSELIER: No.

ME: When do you expect to do that?

DR. BOISSELIER: Soon.

ME: How soon?

DR. BOISSELIER: When the answers that I have been asking to my scientists are clear with the enucleation of cow eggs.

ME: And what are those questions you're asking your scientists?

DR. BOISSELIER: To show me that there is indeed absolutely a very good reproductive activity in the enucleation of the cow.

ME: Great. Now you had just said a few minutes ago that a cow is a different type of mammal than a human.

DR. BOISSELIER: Yes.

ME: So how is it that you're doing the enucleations of the cows and you somehow think that this research will positively affect your research on human cloning?

DR. BOISSELIER: Because we know perfectly the difference between the enucleation of the cow eggs and the enucleation of the human eggs. These have been very well described.

ME: Why are you doing the cow eggs if you know they're different from the human eggs?

DR. BOISSELIER: It's easy to answer. It's difficult and I will not sacrifice any human eggs in the practicing of this technology, so what they are doing today is doing the practicing on cow eggs . . .

ME: . . . I assume your researchers are planning to apply to the FDA for an IND [an Investigational New Drug application form, to determine the safety of a new drug or procedure] for this human research, correct?

DR. BOISSELIER: I've received a letter telling me to do that recently, yes.

ME: So are they going to apply?

DR. BOISSELIER: I will check with my counsel.

ME: You don't know if they are?

DR. BOISSELIER: I just don't know.

ME: Who did you get the letter from, the FDA?

DR. BOISSELIER: The FDA.

ME: So you don't know whether you'll apply or not for doing this human cloning research?

DR. BOISSELIER: I have to review the letter, of course.

ME: Do you think you need to apply?

DR. BOISSELIER: I will review the letter.

ME: When did you get the letter?

DR. BOISSELIER: Yesterday, so I am sorry, I do not have the time to review that.

ME: Well, now here's what the FDA says, and I'm quoting. "Clinical researchers in cloning technology to clone a human being are subject to FDA regulation under the PHS [Public Health Service] Act and the FD&C [Food, Drug and Cosmetic] Act. Before such research could begin, the researcher must submit an IND request to FDA, which FDA would review to determine if such research could proceed. FDA believes that there are major unresolved safety questions on the use of cloning technology to clone a human being and therefore would

not permit any investigation to proceed at this time."
So, do you plan to follow that and apply or not?

DR. BOISSELIER: I will have to ask my counsel . . .

Predictably, Brigitte Boisselier and the Raelians never filed the appropriate paperwork with the FDA but apparently continued with their outlaw approach, outside government guidelines. At least that's what they'd have us believe. Dr. Boisselier surfaced a few years later, in front of a United Nations panel on human cloning, and at this later date alleged that scientists working with her on behalf of the Raelians had successfully cloned thirteen children. Not just one. Not just a couple. But thirteen. And yet no one in Dr. Boisselier's organization would confirm the whereabouts of these children or provide any evidence that the cloning took place as she described. She was nonetheless steadfast in her insistence that the Raelians were well on their way toward achieving their ultimate goal of eternal life.

"The real crime against humanity," she wrote in a letter to UN ambassadors presumably in defense of her group's renegade science, "is to deny people the right to live forever."

Next, we heard from Dr. Zavos, responding to questions concerning the abnormalities in brain function in Dolly the sheep, and the related concern about the health of her unnamed offspring: "We might have to take him to Harvard or something in order to have an IQ and that is really somewhat of an insult to people's intelligence, talking about that," Dr. Zavos said. "That sheep only needs enough brain to graze, and thank God, we know that much."

Dr. Zavos, a professor emeritus of reproductive physiology–andrology at the University of Kentucky, was an ardent supporter of reproductive cloning. Subsequent to our hearing, he claimed at a press conference to have implanted a cloned embryo into a woman's womb. Like the Raelians, he refused to give any additional information but said he filmed the event and would allow DNA testing. Not surprisingly, seven years later, we are still waiting for this evidence.

It would be easy to dismiss the spectacle of Dr. Boisselier and Dr. Zavos and their attempts to clone humans. But as noted by a real international leader in stem cell ethics, Suzi Leather, chairwoman of the Human Fertilization and Embryology Authority (HFEA), the government-appointed organization that regulates treatment and research in the U.K. involving human embryos outside the body: "Zavos's media stunt is more than just a stunt. It has demonstrated that there will always be someone who is willing to exploit patients and go ahead and risk distress and suffering in a child to further their own ends."

I must admit, I found the whole business of that cloning hearing rather amusing, and from a purely sporting standpoint it was even entertaining. But from a public policy standpoint, it was an outrage that the business of government could be co-opted in such an elemental way by a fringe group promoting values and views that sat decidedly outside the norm.

After a while, I turned to Jim Greenwood and asked, "Why did you call this panel? These people are all nuts."

And they were.

I had an enormous amount of respect for Jim. I still do. He has always been on the right side of scientific issues, and after he left Congress he was named CEO of BIO, the trade organization of the biotech industry. Still, I could not imagine what he was thinking when he scheduled the Raelians and Dr. Zavos to be on the first panel of what should have been an important scientific hearing. I think Jim wanted to get the press to focus on the issues surrounding cloning, but the minute Brigitte Boisselier's testimony ended, Rael stood up and marched out of the room, followed by his acolytes *and* all the press. We were left with the legitimate scientists and ethicists who were the next witnesses, and of course no press to cover the debate—so I guess you could say Jim's plan backfired. It turned out to be spectacle for the sake of spectacle, as opposed to spectacle for the sake of highlighting a greater good.

Later on in the hearing, Thomas H. Murray of the National Bioethics Advisory Commission offered compelling testimony that succinctly expressed my point of view, but by the time he spoke the reporters and cameras had all gone. "Now imagine for a minute a new drug that caused abnormalities or neonatal deaths in half of the babies born to the women treated with this new drug," Murray said. "Imagine further that the women themselves, many of them suffered serious harm, and then imagine that the women who are given this drug were otherwise totally healthy. Would we be having a debate about the ethical acceptability of whether this drug should be distributed? Or would we condemn it resoundingly as unethical experimentation on human beings?"

He continued: "What is accomplished, I find myself asking today, by proclamations such as those made by . . . Dr. Zavos and the Raelians? Well, it seems to me two things are clearly accomplished. Number one, you get enormous heaps of free publicity. This is good for business, if that's what you're after. Number two, you provide false hope and possible exploitation of parents, desperate in their grief over having lost a child. One more thing, if people are permitted to go ahead at this time, is that we will have many dead fetuses, probably some damaged women and maybe, but maybe not, a live born child or two who will almost certainly be born with severe abnormalities."

Dr. Bosselier and the Raelians may have raised a couple of eyebrows at that 2001 hearing, and their far-fetched claims fueled the paranoia of those who feared that legitimate SCNT research might lead to legions of clones like something out of a science fiction movie. Most of us in the hearing room were flashing each other the same *are-we-hearing-what-we-think-we're-hearing?* looks I later exchanged with Nancy Pelosi when President Bush started talking about ethical cell-based research and banning reproductive cloning during his last State of the Union address. That's what incredulous looks like, I'm afraid. However, I'm also afraid that our continued incredulity might undermine the very real, very practical, and very responsible advances that await us on the SCNT front—if only we can set our ideology and our ignorance aside and focus on the science at hand.

We are at a crossroads on this issue, and I'll look to HFEA chairwoman Suzi Leather to sum things up: "The UN ban on reproductive cloning is stalled. Many will wonder how much longer it can be delayed. Any ban must be more than a declaration of condemnation. It must be backed up by national regimes capable of enforcing such a ban. With the exception of the U.K., there are currently few countries anywhere in the world with the necessary regulatory regime to do that."

NINE

ABSTINENCE ONLY

You wouldn't believe some of the stuff they're teaching our kids in public school—all in the name of a moral code the religious right is determined to foist on the rest of us.

In 1996, Congress approved an Abstinence-Only Education block grant program that continues to this day, despite studies that show it doesn't work and that the overwhelming majority of Americans don't want anything to do with it.

I can't imagine a more misguided effort—or a more irresponsible use of public funds. And yet for some mysterious reason, abstinence-only sex education is still being taught in our schools, indoctrinating our children with a biblically based approach to human sexuality at a time in their young lives when they should be receiving a balanced stream of science- and fact-based information to help them make informed choices about their behavior. Through 2007, the federal government has spent more than $1.5 billion on this program, which has bought us only a wealth of misinformation and made it ever more difficult for parents to connect with children in a meaningful way on the too-important issues of sex education and birth control.

Remarkably, the United States is the only developed country with a federally funded abstinence-only education program aimed at school-age children—and this alone is telling. When I was growing up, the United States was out in front on a number of progressive initiatives in education and social programming, so why is it that no one else is following our lead on this one?

It should be noted here that federal law does not require sex education in our public schools. It's up to individual states and local school districts to determine their own curricula in this area, or to determine whether they want to teach this material at all. At present, thirty-nine states require at least some minimum level of sex education to be taught in their public schools. Nationwide, more than two out of three school districts mandate some type of sex education, and among this group 51 percent formally encourage abstinence as the preferred option for teenagers considering sexual activity, while at the same time allowing for a more comprehensive course of study that at least considers contraception. If states or local school districts want to receive federal funding to assist them with their sex education programs, however, they must use an abstinence-only curriculum approved by the federal government.

Before I get going on the suspect merits of abstinence-only education, I believe a careful reading of the mandate behind it is appropriate. Be forewarned: Most people reading the requirements think it's either a joke, or some misguided effort to take us back to an "Ozzie and Harriet" age of innocence that never really existed in our country in the first place.

According to Section 510 of the Social Security Act:

A Title V Abstinence Education program (1) has, as its exclusive purpose, teaching the social, psychological, and health gains of abstaining from sexual activity; (2) teaching abstinence from sexual activity outside of marriage as the expected standard for all school-age children; (3) teaching that abstinence is the only certain way to avoid out-of-wedlock pregnancy, STDs, and associated health problems; (4) teaching that a mutually faithful monogamous relationship within marriage is the expected standard of human sexual activity; (5) teaching that sexual activity outside of marriage is likely to have harmful psychological and physical effects; (6) teaching that bearing children out-of-wedlock is likely to have harmful consequences for the child, the child's parents, and society; (7) teaching young people how to reject sexual advances and how alcohol and drug use increases vulnerability to sexual advances; and (8) teaching the importance of attaining self-sufficiency before engaging in sex.

While many of the goals stated in the guidelines are admirable, they are not science-based. And the most terrifying piece is that a good and appropriate idea—namely, to encourage teenagers to abstain from sex while at the same time arming them with the information they'll need if they chose to become sexually active—has been perverted to reflect a narrow religious view that leaves our children exposed to disease and unwanted pregnancy, among other disasters.

It also calls into question our federal budget priorities. At a February 2007 Energy and Commerce Committee hearing on the FY2008 HHS budget, for example, Congresswoman Lois Capps of California, a registered nurse, noted with great concern that the president's budget cut funding for nursing education by nearly one-third, from $150 million to $105.3 million, while increasing the proposed budget for abstinence-only education programs to more than $200 million. This, said Lois, for an "unproven, scientifically inaccurate program that lacks oversight."

Over the years, the abstinence-only initiative has struck a great many of us on Capitol Hill as a waste of our tax dollars and an overreaching of our role as keepers of the public trust, to put in place a curriculum that decries pre-marital sex as the root of all societal ills and to advance a single set of religious beliefs. The Christian conservative lobby struck fear into both Republican leaders and Democrats from Bible-belt states who really didn't want to talk about these issues in their re-election campaigns. Few in Washington wanted to stand up and publicly recognize that teenagers might actually have sex, even if we told them not to.

At the abstinence-only core was a *Just Say No!* approach to sex education, which fundamentalists believed was the surest way to prevent pregnancy and sexually transmitted diseases. Unfortunately, such a limited view also prevented science-based sex education, because it's impossible to teach teenagers about sex if we ask them first to stick their heads in the sand.

To religious conservatives, the abstinence-only education program was merely a first step toward an admitted effort to keep our children from engaging in sexual activity outside the holy bonds of matrimony. One such conservative, George W. Bush, pledged during his 2000 presidential campaign to redouble our efforts in abstinence-only education by increasing federal spending and improving the core curriculum materials made available to teachers—so even though the program didn't start on his watch it appeared from the outset that it would thrive in a Bush administration.

Abstinence-only sex education has been around since the Reagan administration. In 1981, Congress first passed the Adolescent Family Life Act (AFLA), without any committee deliberation or floor debate, as part of the Omnibus Budget Reconciliation

Act. (These omnibus bills are often the source of great mischief, because they're rammed through in the wee hours of the morning at the end of the congressional session. They're thousands of pages long, and nobody really knows what's in them, because the staffs finish drafting them only minutes before we vote on them.) The purpose of AFLA was to give grants to non-profit organizations to establish "family centered" programs to assist pregnant and parenting teens in developing "chastity" and "self-discipline." This program is still being funded, to the tune of $13 million in our current budget.

In 1996, with the passage of the Welfare Reform Act, the federal government really got into abstinence-only in a big way. That was the year the new Republican Congress and the Clinton White House appropriated $50 million per year for states to teach abstinence-only as part of their sex education programs. At first, the requirements of the act did allow states some curricular flexibility, but after the 2000 elections these requirements were severely tightened.

Under the leadership of the Republican Congress and President Bush, funding for the abstinence-only program has been dramatically increased, while the program itself has been narrowed in scope. In 2000, Congress created a program—authorized under Title XI of the Social Security Act—that funded abstinence-only programs at an astonishing level of $60 million. Over the years, that number has grown, to $176 million in 2007. A proposed increase of $38 million for FY2008 in the Marriage and Healthy Family Development Initiative budget was eventually trimmed to match FY2007 levels.

Recently, there has been a lot of push-back against abstinence-only programs from states and sex education scholars who point out that, intuitively and as a matter of research, these programs not only don't work but can do more harm than good. Additionally, they siphon money from other health care and education initiatives that *do* work and are sorely needed. More than that, they run counter to the prevailing notion that our schools ought to be in the business of teaching facts, not opinions. And yet here we are, all these years later, and abstinence-only won't go away.

Studies showing that abstinence-only doesn't work continue to mount. One Texas A&M evaluation of five abstinence-only programs being taught in Texas schools reported that students in virtually all high school grades were *more* sexually active after taking the course! And according to a comprehensive evaluation commissioned by Congress, conducted by Mathematica, Inc. and released in April, 2007, teenagers who participated in abstinence-only education programs had just as many sexual partners as teenagers who had not participated in the program. Abstinence-only kids were no more likely to abstain from sex than other kids.

Granted, $176 million is not a lot of money in the grand scheme of our federal budget, but I find it interesting that defenders of abstinence-only always point to the fact that it's not a lot of money as an argument in favor of continuing the effort. That's hokum. To those who look on $176 million as some kind of drop-in-the-bucket, perhaps I should suggest a redrafting of our math curricula as well. On a per-school basis, the abstinence-only budget works out to a few thousand dollars per school, and that's certainly a meaningful number. Just think what you could do with that kind of money. You could buy textbooks and supplies. You could start a computer lab. You could fund a new program—one that's rooted in scientific fact, instead of ideological fantasy. You could actually do things. They might not be huge things, in terms of furthering someone's social agenda, but you could make a difference with that kind of money.

Because of the severe curricular strings attached to the money, a growing number of states have chosen to reject the funds—even though their schools are strapped for cash and can use all the federal dollars they can get their hands on. At present, sixteen states reject abstinence-only funding: Arizona, Colorado, Connecticut, Maine, Massachusetts, Minnesota, Montana, New Jersey, New Mexico, New York, Ohio, Rhode Island, Virginia, Wisconsin and Wyoming, along with California, the only state that has never accepted federal funding for this initiative.

At the grassroots level, family planning advocates have become angry and frustrated at the constraints under which they must operate. During the 2006 mid-term election campaign, I found myself talking to a community group in northeast Denver about what the Democrats hoped to accomplish if we took back the House of Representatives. During the Q&A session at the end of my talk, a woman raised her hand and said, "Whatever you do, zero out that God-awful abstinence-only program."

I agreed with her, but at the same time I was startled by her vehemence. The woman went on to tell me that she worked as a counselor in a center for unwed mothers—and, because the center received federal monies for its sex education programs, she was required to teach abstinence-only.

She said, "Here I am, talking to a roomful of pregnant women or women who have just had babies, telling them not to have sex before they get married. I'm sorry, but that horse has already left the barn!"

As a parent of teenage girls, I can certainly appreciate the impulse to teach our children about abstinence. We want our kids to make good, responsible choices, and we certainly don't want them to grow up too fast. Indeed, it is difficult to argue the point that abstinence might be "the only certain way" to avoid pregnancy and sexually transmitted diseases, but who are we in Congress to set an expected standard of behavior for our school-age children? Forgive me, but I'd always thought those were the kinds of values that get handed down and decided upon within families and communities, not mandated by government. And who are we to withhold valuable pieces of information from our children, just because we want to fill their heads with religious ideology in such a way that there's no room left for facts and science-based strategies that might actually do them some good?

Even more troubling than the misspent funds is the misplaced message we're sending to our teenagers, drawn from the right-wing religious bias of the federally funded curricula. If you look closely at some of these classroom materials, you'll find poorly written textbooks that misrepresent the effectiveness of condoms, contain wildly inaccurate information about abortion, and spend far more time proselytizing about chastity and fidelity than educating students about basic human biology. You'll find supposedly educational videos that threaten our kids with the fear of God and eternal damnation and hellfire and whatever else these supposed educators can think to throw into the mix, just to keep our kids chaste. And here's what you won't find: a fair-minded, open-ended dialogue, or an environment in which our children might voice concerns about their sexuality and the difficult choices they are confronted with on a daily basis.

Here's one particularly thoughtful response to a student foolish enough to ask what would happen if she chose to have sex before marriage, from a video called *No Second Chance:* "Well I guess you just have to be prepared to die. And you'll probably take with you your spouse and one or more of your children . . ."

Here's another gem, from a textbook called *Sex Respect:* "If pre-marital sex came in a bottle, it would probably have to carry a Surgeon General's warning, something like the one on a package of cigarettes. There's no way to have pre-marital sex without hurting someone."

And it's not just the heavy-handed opinions that should have us worried; it's the unconscionable spread of distorted information that is presented as fact:

- one text describes a fetus of forty-three days old as "a thinking person";

- one book explains that a child is conceived when twenty-four chromosomes from the mother join with twenty-four chromosomes from the father (the correct number is twenty-three);

- and, several volumes offer misinformation about the risks of abortion, suggesting that 5 to 10 percent of women who have legal abortions will become sterile, and that the risk of premature birth and tubal and cervical pregnancies will increase following the abortion of a first pregnancy, despite the fact that there are no such risks associated with commonly practiced abortion procedures.

Some of this misleading information is deeply disturbing, such as the way every discussion of abortion is cloaked with shades of gloom and doom, but other errors and inconsistencies are laughable. In one course outline, it is presented as a statement of fact that touching your partner's genitals "can result in pregnancy." In another, you can find the contention that "remaining a virgin all but eliminates the possibility of becoming pregnant."

You can't make this stuff up—well . . . actually, you *can*. God knows, that's what these people are doing, and they're doing it with the federal government's approval and funding.

There's also a concerted effort in the abstinence-only curricula to create or perpetrate traditional stereotypes about boys and girls and to present them as scientific facts. And underneath all the psycho-babble there's an alarming amount of valuable and necessary information—on birth control, abortion and safe sex—that simply doesn't get discussed at all.

One series of textbooks published through this program is particularly offensive. The series is called *Choosing the Best,* and it purports to help students make good, positive decisions regarding their relationships. As such, it seems more appropriate for Sunday School than public school, but these textbooks are turning up in schools with federal funding all across the country. In one, students are asked to read a meandering fable about a princess and a knight and a dragon. (Keep in mind, this is a sex education textbook intended for a *public* high school audience.) In the fable, the knight repeatedly rescues the fair princess from the dragon, by various means, each of which is suggested by the princess. There's one encounter involving poison, and another involving a noose, and on and on. The knight vanquishes the dragon each time, but he always leaves the castle feeling a little bit ashamed that this damsel-in-distress must invariably tell him what to do. He would like to be more in charge. He would like the princess to give him more of a chance to discover these things for himself, to stand on his own. But, alas, this does not happen. Finally, the knight loses interest in the princess. He meets and marries a village maiden, after determining that she knows nothing about slaying dragons, or poison, or nooses, and together they live happily ever after.

The lesson for our young people? Well, the textbook authors tell us the fable is meant to remind teenage girls that it's okay to offer occasional suggestions and assistance to the teenage boys in their life, but also to remember that too much assertiveness will lessen the boy's confidence and drive him away from his princess.

It's enough to make you lose your school lunch.

In another textbook, there's a distressingly arcane reference to traditional wedding customs. "The father gives the bride to the groom because he is the one man who has had the responsibility of protecting her throughout her life," the book's authors assert. "He is now giving his daughter to the only other man who will take over this protective role."

In still another textbook, it is suggested that men seek "admiration" from their female partners, while women seek "financial support." Continuing . . . "Just as a woman needs to feel a man's devotion to her, a man has a primary need to feel a woman's admiration. To admire a man is to regard him with wonder, delight and approval. A man feels admired when his unique characteristics and talents happily amaze her."

What are our young people to make of this? And what does a discussion of stereotypical gender roles, however misguided, have to do with abstinence in the first place?

The abstinence-only message echoes throughout our government-backed education initiatives outside the classroom—as in the one-sided message a not-so-careful reader might find between the lines of information pages posted on the website www.4parents.gov, a resource intended to foster dialogue between parent and child on issues relating to teenage sexuality. The site is administered by the Department of Health & Human Services, written and maintained by the Office of Public Health and Science, and funded by our tax dollars, so visitors might reasonably expect to receive straightforward, useful information, offered without bias or agenda.

Or then again, they might not.

In a section entitled "Teen Pregnancy," parents and teenagers are encouraged to consider the consequences of an unwanted pregnancy. "If a teen girl finds out she is pregnant," the section begins, "she and her parents, and the father of the baby and his parents have some tough decisions to make. None of them are easy."

The section goes on to detail the various options available to unwed teenage mothers, but it presents these options in a loaded, one-sided manner that smells more like a scolding lecture than a clinical analysis.

Consider:

> Some teen mothers decide to continue their pregnancy and then choose adoption for their baby. Adoption may be the best choice for the baby and the teen parents. There are many adoption agencies and types of adoption. Some teens are able to meet the parents who wish to adopt the baby.

What's interesting here is that carrying the child to term and offering it for adoption is presented as an option of first resort—almost like a default option. Indeed, it may be "the best choice," as the website strongly suggests, leaving no room for an opposing point of view. Alarmingly, there is no mention of the various complications of pregnancy, just as there is no mention of the social difficulties the teenage mother could expect to experience if she chooses to continue the pregnancy. The language used to describe this option is warm, supportive, and comforting.

As the "lecture" continues, the language grows a little more judgmental:

> *Many teens decide to keep their babies. Some marry the baby's father and raise their baby together. Sometimes the baby's grandparents or other family members help raise it so that the teen mother can stay in school and work. But it requires a lot of additional hard work for a teen parent to finish school and get a good job. Children of teen mothers face greater risk of poverty, behavioral problems, poor academic performance, incarceration, and teen pregnancy, so good parenting skills are very important.*

Here, too, there is cause for alarm. The hidden message to this second option is that, if a teenager mother decides to keep her baby and raise it herself, that child will wind up in jail or on drugs. The language used to describe this second, less-desirable option is a whole lot less warm and fuzzy. It's reproving and harsh. It suggests that the teenage mother had been headed down some kind of wrong road, and that her unborn child will be headed down that same wrong road before long.

Finally, the website comes to abortion, the option of last resort:

> *Some teen pregnancies end in abortion. Abortions can have complications. There may be emotional consequences, as well. Some women say that they feel sad and some use more alcohol or drugs than before.*

Now the language has become incendiary, tying abortion to drug and alcohol use, although previously there had been no mention of depression or dependency in relation to carrying the pregnancy to term, and there have been no studies to determine any type of causal link between abortion and depression or dependency. Furthermore, the site's writers *never* mention that a pregnancy carried to term carries more health risks than an abortion, or the fact that post-partum depression is a proven diagnosis, where there is no evidence of increased depression following abortion. And yet the site's writers and administrators present this statement as established fact, no doubt in hopes of discouraging young women from even considering terminating their pregnancies.

I don't mean to suggest here that our government should promote abortion over other choices for unwed mothers. Not at all. I do think, however, that a government-sponsored website should be medically accurate and nonjudgmental. I'm afraid the www.4parents.gov site fails on both counts.

Abstinence-only was one of the first issues we looked at when the Democrats regained control of Congress in January 2007. As co-chair of the Pro-Choice Caucus, I said that this program had to go. Cutting funds for abstinence-only was one of our priorities, and our thinking was clear: Abstinence-only was emblematic of the closed-minded worldview of the religious right and a disconcerting reminder of a time when Christian conservatives held our elected officials hostage to their fundamentalist ideals. Plus, it didn't work. But—so far, at least—we haven't been able to move abstinence-only off the table. Our leadership reported that the president had threatened to veto the entire Labor, Health & Human Services appropriations bill if we eliminated abstinence-only. Over the objection of the Pro-Choice Caucus and advocacy groups, the Democratic leaders decided that this was a fight they didn't want to take on just yet, so we backed off for the time being.

What we didn't anticipate was that the bill the Appropriations Committee brought to the floor would propose an *increase* in abstinence-only funding—a whopping 33 percent increase in just one of the programs! We Democrats were furious over this. It's one thing to let the program continue so the entire bill would not be vetoed, but it's another matter entirely to increase spending in this area, especially when Congress was trying to tighten spending and had instituted a pay-as-you-go policy.

Fortunately, we were ultimately able to hold the line on spending. It was a victory, sort of. Unfortunately, it's not just the president who continues to push for this program. Abstinence-only didn't start with George W. Bush, and from the looks of things it won't end with him either. There are quite a few members of Congress who really believe in the message of abstinence—such as Rep. Chris Smith (R-New Jersey), who it sometimes seems has made it his full and absolute mission to advance the message of the Catholic Church throughout our government. He's against birth control. He's against sex outside of marriage. We've had a number of heated floor debates on these issues, and I always get the feeling he looks on me as the handmaiden of the devil. In an unguarded moment, he might tell you I'm partially responsible for killing unborn babies. These are the kinds of people we're dealing with in Congress, so change will take some time.

I was hoping the new Mathematica study would give us some of the muscle we needed to fight back on abstinence-only, but apparently those hopes were unfounded under the Bush administration. This became apparent soon enough and was reinforced for me time and time again. In March 2008, at a hearing on the administration's budget, I asked Secretary Leavitt why his proposed budget sought to increase funding for abstinence-only sex education programs by $28 million when the Mathematica study had stated quite clearly that "the impact results from the four selected programs show no impact on the rates of sexual activity."

It's a reasonable question, wouldn't you agree?

At first, Secretary Leavitt argued that the Mathematica study was open to interpretation, and then he insisted that he could make improvements to the program. I've yet to hear what those improvements might be—perhaps teaching *abstinence-based* sex education—but I'm not holding out any great hope.

Realize, those of us on the side of reason on this issue are not suggesting we shouldn't teach abstinence. Here again, that's not the case at all. I wholeheartedly believe we should encourage our children to abstain from sex until marriage, but at the same time we should also teach them the science of birth control; abstinence should most definitely be the first focus of the message we're putting out to children, but it just shouldn't be the entire message.

And yet abstinence-only has become a hot-button issue that too many candidates are afraid to address. It's almost untouchable. It bumps up against all kinds of related issues like abortion and birth control. It makes people squeamish, and so they shy from talking about it.

That's the kind of backward thinking we're still dealing with in some of our elected officials. On a backward-thinking initiative like abstinence-only sex education, we need to bring the full force of our forward-thinking counterargument in order to turn things around.

To paraphrase Dr. Martin Luther King Jr., my hero, I have a dream that someday we will be able to talk about sex education like rational adults, and that we will institute and fund science-based programs that deter teens from having early and ill-advised sex, while still preparing them for the challenges they will face in this twenty-first century.

The best part about this dream is that it seems attainable. The worst part? In our current political landscape, it also seems hopelessly unrealistic.

TEN

WHATEVER IT IS, I'M AGAINST IT!

One of the chief objections to science-based sex education has been the erroneous claim that condoms do not protect against the human papillomavirus—a constellation of sexually transmitted diseases commonly known as HPV, which can cause genital warts or pre-cancerous lesions and in many cases can lead to cervical cancer. Opponents of comprehensive sex education have long asserted that, because people cannot be completely protected from all STDs, the only foolproof way to be safe is abstinence.

I've always believed it was unreasonable and somewhat irresponsible to presume that encouraging young people to say *no* to sex was enough to prevent them from having sex or from getting sexually transmitted diseases. The anti–sex education crowd seems to have forgotten about human nature. While it's true that condoms don't fully eliminate the risk of all STDs, it's also true that when used properly they greatly reduce the risk of disease and unwanted pregnancy. Some studies report that proper condom use can reduce the risk of HIV/AIDS by as much as 99 percent, and it seems to me a far more productive course of action and a sounder public policy to advocate proper condom use than to simply tell our young people to abstain from sex and then hope for the best.

This is serious business when it comes to the spread of HPV—one of the leading risk factors in nearly all cases of cervical cancer, the leading cause of cancer death among women in the developed world, and the second most common type of cancer among women worldwide. It's serious business, too, in the protection against HIV/AIDS, which has killed more than 16 million people worldwide. And yet we've allowed the Christian conservative agenda to put people at risk by ignoring initiatives that make condoms more readily available and understood.

I never could figure out the objection to condoms as a means to reduce the risk of sexually transmitted disease in the first place, but at least the religious right's position on HPV is consistent with its dogma against all pre-marital sexual activity and its rejection of all forms of birth control. And because the right wing's objections were at least consistent, I never gave them much thought—except to mumble under my breath at the absurdity of this position, given the enormous risks involved, and to shudder at the weight these objections carried in certain parts of the country. That is, I didn't give them much thought until a number of my colleagues across the aisle started talking about the misuse or overuse of condoms in general and railing against the promotion of condoms as a preventive measure against HPV, HIV, and other STDs. After all, it's one thing to hold an opinion that runs counter to accepted research; it's quite another thing to leap-frog your opinion over accepted research and force it upon the general public. But that's how these people operate. They stand behind a blatant falsehood and use that position as the basis for an argument in support of another obvious deceit. That's been my take on the Republican case against science-based sex education all along, because it's beyond me how any logical, thoughtful, *reasonable* person could argue against science. The facts are the facts. The research is the research. Everything else is conjecture or personal opinion, and there's little room for either in a discussion on public health.

The voices of protest all sounded the same theme on this one—that condoms could not protect our young people from disease, and that abstinence was the only way to ensure continued health. Consider this neat little condom-condemnation, from my former colleague Jo Ann Davis (R-Virginia): "We're sending the wrong message when we use taxpayer dollars to give condoms out to these kids and we don't tell them, 'By the way, you'll probably be dead at age twenty-four by cervical cancer. But we're giving you condoms, so go do your thing.' To me, abstinence is the only way."

Religious conservatives even went so far as to call for warning labels to be affixed to condom packages—alerting potential users that condoms do *not*, in fact, eliminate the risk of sexually transmitted disease. I guess they figure this will get people thinking they were treading in some kind of potentially fatal territory. I heard this and thought, *Warning labels on condom packages? What in God's name will these people think of next?*

Tom Coburn, an Oklahoma doctor-turned-congressman (now serving in the U.S. Senate) who had once been a deacon of his Baptist church, was a member of our committee, and his was one of the loudest, most reproachful voices against condoms. Like a lot of right-leaning, middle-aged men, Senator Coburn tended to ooze a kind of oily concern for the young women of America. If you didn't notice his concern at first, he'd be sure to lecture you about it. I don't know about you, but I always get a little spooked when somebody tells me he's got my best interests at heart and then goes and acts in a way that has nothing to do with my best interests. The fact that Senator Coburn happened to be a medical doctor as well as a member of Congress brought the weight of the medical profession on his comments—which, of course, was a whole different kind of scary.

Whenever I listened to a guy like Tom Coburn, my skin would start to crawl and I'd get to thinking, *Oh my God, what if I had a guy like* that *as my doctor?* He was known on Capitol Hill for the graphic slide show he presented to young Congressional staffers, featuring shots of untreated venereal diseases and misleading statistics about the ineffectiveness of condoms. Those efforts mostly elicited chuckles and eye-rolling from members of Congress. But because Senator Coburn was a member of the Energy and Commerce Committee, he had a soapbox for trying to insert his views into actual legislation.

In our committee hearings, Senator Coburn stated repeatedly that he was opposed to the promotion of condoms as a guard against sexually transmitted disease, primarily because they had not been shown to prevent the spread of HPV. He kept reminding everybody that he was a doctor and that he knew what he was talking about—but he didn't sound like a doctor and he didn't sound like he knew what he was talking about. His comments were laced with alarmist rhetoric and convoluted thinking. He even referenced an unnamed study that reported that the incidence of cervical cancer among nuns was zero, presumably to reinforce his point that abstinence was the only sure way to avoid HPV.

Senator Coburn's big idea was to put a "black box" label on condom packages, warning that condoms did not offer protection against HPV. A black box label is the highest-level of alert available to the Food and Drug Administration, which has oversight on the distribution of condoms, which are considered a "medical device." It's like a threat level of red, or severe, issued by the Department of Homeland Security, only here the presumed threat was to our public health and our moral responsibility to do right by the American people. The warning labels would be akin to the Surgeon General's warning box that tobacco companies are required to place on the sides of cigarette packaging, saying that cigarettes can kill you. The black box designation means the warning would actually be entombed in a black box on the outside of the condom package, and not placed on a folded-over warning sheet inserted into the package, stating the risks and benefits of the product. There would be no mistaking it, no avoiding it, no designing it in such a way that it could look anything but alarming.

Senator Coburn was like a dog with a bone on this one. He just wouldn't let it go. He introduced legislation on condom labeling in the late 1990s, and when that didn't fly he offered amendments on the House floor in favor of this warning label. He offered amendments in committee. He even used the issue to try to block the nomination of controversial FDA Commissioner Lester Crawford, because of his support of condom use. Senator Coburn took his argument from the House to the Senate, arguing as forcefully as he could for this black box warning, which his opponents believed would only confuse the consumer, because of course most folks have no idea what HPV is, or how it's transmitted, or how it can affect you. This last point suggests a whole separate argument that we need to do more to educate people on the danger and prevalence of HPV and its relation to cervical cancer, but for our purposes here it merely suggests a huge and troubling disconnect. Most right-minded people could tell you what would happen if we slapped such a dire-looking label on each and every condom package: People would just look at these warning labels and think that if they used condoms they'd get sick.

I saw this warning label push as nothing more than a ploy to get the American public not to use condoms, which of course was precisely what people like Tom Coburn wanted. And yet condom labeling remains under review by the FDA as of this writing, thanks to the aggressive lobbying of the religious right. Senator Coburn is still making noise about this, and I suspect he will continue to make noise until he has his way or until the issue is finally resolved.

But it doesn't end with warning labels. Throughout President Bush's first term in office, the Republican majority orchestrated an effort to remove important public health information from websites administered by the Centers for Disease Control and Prevention (CDC) and the National Cancer Institute (NCI), including a fact sheet on the proper use of condoms. I'll address the NCI omissions elsewhere in these pages, but the misinformation on the CDC site struck a group of House Democrats as such an outrageous abuse of power and authority that we wrote a letter to HHS Secretary Tommy Thompson to state our objections. I was joined in this effort by my colleagues Henry Waxman, Sherrod Brown, Nita Lowey, Rosa DeLauro, Diane Watson, Bernard Sanders, Edolphus Towns, Carolyn Maloney, William Lacy Clay, Elijah Cummings, Tom Allen, and Dennis Kucinich. Specifically, we objected to the removal from the CDC website of a fact sheet entitled "Condoms and Their Use in Preventing HIV Infection and Other STDs." Generally, we balked at the use of these websites to promote any kind of agenda, because a great many Americans utilized them as a resource of first resort when seeking guidance on health-related matters.

Secretary Thompson responded quickly to our letter. He explained that the fact sheet had been taken down because some of the information it contained had become out of date. We took him at his word, but continued to monitor the CDC website to keep the secretary honest. Sure enough, a couple weeks later a revised fact sheet was posted, under the heading "Fact Sheet for Public Health Personnel: Male Latex Condoms and Sexually Transmitted Diseases." It was a bit bewildering that this new fact sheet was directed only at public health personnel, and not at the general public, but I looked past that bit of strangeness and focused instead on the information the revised website contained—or, rather, the information it no longer contained. This was beyond bewildering; it was downright disturbing. The original fact sheet had stated that "the primary reason that condoms sometimes fail to prevent HIV/STD infection or pregnancy is incorrect or inconsistent use, not failure of the condoms itself." It then went on to describe five steps for effective condom use. However, the revised fact sheet carried no information on effective condom use. Presumably, this was the information that Secretary Thompson and his staff had determined was out of date.

The original fact sheet had also contained information on the usefulness of various types of condoms, including a detailed description of different products and information on how effective they were in preventing HIV/STD transmission. For example, the fact sheet explained that lambskin or "novelty" condoms should not be counted on to protect against disease. There was also information on synthetic condoms for people who were allergic to latex. In the revised fact sheet, however, there was no such information on alternative condom types, which we argued made it more difficult for people relying exclusively on the CDC to help them make educated choices about which condoms were effective or appropriate. Here again, we could only assume that this useful material was now also considered archaic by the right-leaning minds at the CDC.

Elsewhere in that same letter to Secretary Thompson, we expressed concern about the removal from the CDC site of a discussion on the role of condoms in encouraging or discouraging teenagers to engage in sexual activity. As originally posted, the fact sheet concluded that there was no evidence that condom use had any impact on the timing of a young couple's decision to have intercourse for the first time. Now, with the Bush White House maintaining that condom use promoted increased teenage sexual activity, despite scientific studies to the contrary, this information was mysteriously expunged from the site—apparently because it too had been found "out of date," or at the very least "out of fashion" with an administration that now openly opposed the use of condoms, even for HIV/STD prevention, because the president believed they promoted teenage sex.

"We are extremely concerned about these alterations and deletions of important scientific information," we wrote in the letter's conclusion. "They appear to be part of an Orwellian trend at HHS. Simply put, information that used to be based on science is being systematically removed from the public when it conflicts with the administration's political agenda. We urge you to stop this subversion of science and suppression of information. Your job should be to make sure that people who visit the CDC and NCI websites are fully informed—not to limit their access to vital health information."

This far-reaching miseducation effort flowing from the Bush White House troubles me a great deal. I actually lose sleep over it. Each time the issue surfaces, in its various forms, I cringe at the realization that we are being held hostage by an inane back-and-forth on a matter of such critical importance to the health of our sexually active young people. And yet for the most part the effort never really goes anywhere, because in the end it's all just a lot of hot air and most mainstream Americans are smart enough to see through the mumbo-jumbo.

But as many of us remember from high school chemistry, hot air has an irritating tendency to rise. In September 2006, the *New England Journal of Medicine* reported that condoms *do* in fact reduce the risk of HPV. It was a fairly conclusive, comprehensive report that I hoped would finally give the lie to these ridiculous anti-condom claims. Planned Parenthood issued a press release trumpeting these findings, hoping to quash some of the backward thinking being put out by the religious right that continued to question the efficacy of condoms, while the mainstream press announced the findings with great fanfare. This was certainly a welcome development; but here again, religious conservatives were able to read between the lines and insert their own opinions in place of the research.

There were other welcome developments to come, including the announcement of a first-of-its-kind cancer vaccine that has been proven effective in combating the most dangerous strains of HPV, the ones known to cause almost all cervical cancers. This was a huge breakthrough. There's no overstating it. The vaccine blocks initial infection of the most common sexually transmitted strands of HPV and shows real promise in the fight against cervical cancer. It's as near to an absolute preventative as we can expect on this front, because of course the vaccine can't block infection after the fact, which means that in order for it to be most effective the inoculation must be administered to girls in late adolescence, around the age of eleven or twelve, *before* they become sexually active.

Certainly, we thought, the breakthrough would be well received on both sides of the aisle, because those of us in the legislative fight on health-related issues are all ultimately seeking the same goal—the well-being of the general public. And besides, who could oppose a safe and effective vaccine? Well, as it played out, the religious conservatives found a reason to object to this vaccine as well.

Tony Perkins, a leading Louisiana conservative and president of the Family Research Council, a Christian group that promotes the values of marriage and family, announced in response that he would not give the vaccine to his own daughter. His reason? She might be more inclined to have sex outside marriage. "It sends the wrong message," he said.

It also sent the wrong message to Leslie Unruh, executive director of the National Abstinence Clearinghouse, who said, "I personally object to vaccinating children against a disease that is one hundred percent preventable with proper sexual behavior."

Initially, there was concern about what the CDC's Advisory Committee on Immunization Practices (ACIP) would do about the HPV vaccine. The ACIP sets policy and standards for doctors and health insurance companies regarding the public funding of vaccinations—and for a while it seemed to side with the religious right on this issue. The ACIP recommendations are not binding, but individual states look to ACIP guidelines to determine which vaccines should be required of children before enrolling in school. This was a serious and immediate worry, because the Bush administration had stacked the ACIP with well-known Christian conservatives, including Reginald Finger, who until September 2005 had been the "medical issues analyst" at Focus on the Family, a leading evangelical group.

For the first time in a long while, science seemed to prevail. In June 2006, the ACIP recommended that the new HPV vaccine be routinely given to girls before the onset of sexual activity, and that even sexually active women younger than 26 would benefit from the vaccine. Finally, in January 2007, these recommendations became official CDC policy, and the HPV vaccine is now included in the recommended pediatric immunization schedule.

The scientific community's acceptance of the HPV vaccine has not deterred the religious right in its opposition, however. The hue and cry against this breakthrough vaccine was unfathomable, but at the same time I'm afraid it wasn't that hard to believe. Katha Pollitt, writing in *The Nation,* accurately reflected the absurdity of the objections when she wrote, "Raise your hand if you think that what is keeping girls virgins now is the threat of getting cervical cancer when they are sixty from a disease they've probably never heard of."

Thankfully, the HPV vaccine has not been called into question in Congress—and hopefully, it never will. It has, however, became a critical issue in our state legislatures. In Texas, for example, the legislature determined that the vaccine would be mandatory. After the Republican governor signed the measure into law, there was a firestorm of objection, not just in Texas but across the country. People didn't like the fact that the government was requiring U.S. citizens to medically safeguard their children against one of the unfortunate realities of sexual activity when they felt perfectly capable of safeguarding their children themselves, by expressly forbidding sexual activity.

So let's recap: First, the conservatives objected to condoms because they said they might promote sexual promiscuity. This turned out not to be the case. Then they objected to condoms because they said they are ineffective in preventing the transmission of HIV and other sexually transmitted diseases. This turned out not to be the case. After that, they couched their objections in more specific terms, claiming that condoms had not been shown to protect users from HPV. This too turned out not to be the case. Not only that, but scientists then developed a revolutionary vaccine that effectively eliminated the risk of HPV and, along with it, certain types of cervical cancer, but conservatives found a reason to object to this as well—because they believed it gave young people a false sense of security and perhaps lifted the fear of a life-threatening illness from their arsenal of arguments against pre-marital sex.

I came to realize, if it isn't one thing, it's another. In fact, the entire back-and-forth on this anti-condom/HPV issue reminded me of that great song from *Horsefeathers*. In the movie, Groucho Marx played a small-time college president named Quincy Adams Wagstaff; in one of the first scenes, he gathers with a group of professors in full academic robes and mortarboards and bursts into inexplicable song.

He sings:

> *I don't know what they have to say,*
> *It makes no difference anyway . . .*
> *Whatever it is, I'm against it!*

ELEVEN

AN OUNCE OF PREVENTION

The mixed messages of the religious right on sex and science extend to matters of birth control, where my conservative colleagues have gone on record with ill-considered opinions, half-baked notions, and self-serving positions that invariably leave me questioning their ability to think clearly, let alone serve in elected office.

It's always something, as Gilda Radner used to say—most of it maddening to me and my fair-minded colleagues. We need look no further than the unfortunate decision by Rep. Tom DeLay (R-Texas), in the wake of the tragic Columbine shootings just outside my district in Denver, to read into the record a letter written to a Texas newspaper seeking to understand the massacre. He did so, presumably, because he agreed with the writer's sentiment, which sought to place blame for the shootings on a societal level. "For the life of me," the majority leader read, "I can't understand what could have gone wrong in Littleton, Colorado. If only parents had kept their children away from the guns, we wouldn't have had such a tragedy. Yeah, it must have been the guns . . . It couldn't have been because we have sterilized and contracepted our families down to sizes so small that the children we do have are so spoiled with material things that they come to equate the receiving of the material thing with love."

I'm sure the grieving parents in Littleton, Colorado, were comforted to know that the House majority leader blamed the deaths of their loved ones on contraception. As strange as the connection between gun violence and birth control may seem, though, that's how some religious conservatives look at the world. We're all entitled to our own points of view, I guess, even though the Bush administration would have us believe otherwise.

Certainly, one of the most preposterous and insidious ways the Bush White House has tried to force its anti-science views on an unsuspecting public has been through appointments to high-level Executive Branch positions. In the fall of 2007, for example, the White House announced the appointment of a woman to head the family planning office at HHS who was publicly critical of contraception.

I immediately joined with Louise Slaughter and organized a group of thirty members of Congress (including sixteen women) to send a letter to HHS Secretary Leavitt urging him to reconsider the appointment and to name an appropriately principled individual to the just-vacated post of deputy assistant secretary for the Office of Population Affairs. It seemed to us that the position called for someone who at the very least was committed to family planning and women's health issues. Dr. Susan Orr, Bush's questionable choice for this position, didn't fit the bill on either front and was a well-known adversary of family planning advocates. In April 2001, for example, when President Bush proposed eliminating contraceptive coverage for federal employees, she was fairly outspoken with her approval. "We're quite pleased," she told the *Washington Post*, "because fertility is not a disease. It's not a medical necessity that you have it."

It's difficult to imagine the level of arrogance it takes to put a person with that point of view in charge of the government's Title X Family Planning Program, which provides high-quality family planning and health care to low-income or uninsured individuals and oversees nearly $300 million in annual grants to offer contraceptive services, counseling, and preventive screenings to patients who might not have access to these services.

"Talk about the fox guarding the hen house," I said in a press release, criticizing the appointment, which was not subject to Senate approval.

Readers will not be surprised to learn that our letter didn't accomplish a thing. Secretary Leavitt did not, in fact, reconsider Dr. Orr's appointment. Unbelievably, though, Dr. Orr was not the first anti–birth control activist to be named to lead the family planning office. Her appointment followed the resignation of another Christian conservative from the same post—Eric Keroack, who had been a supervising physician for a Christian pregnancy-counseling organization called A Woman's Concern. Dr. Keroack opposed abortion and pre-marital sex, once comparing the latter to drug use.

It's unthinkable to me that you could find not just one but two people who were publicly opposed to birth control to head up the very agency in charge of family planning for the U.S. government, but that's just what the Bush White House managed to do.

The Orr and Keroack appointments were just two cases of the president stacking agencies and advisory councils with like-minded individuals, presumably to avoid policies not in keeping with his overarching religious views. Another glaring example of the politicization of an agency meant to advise the president on sensitive issues relating to sex and reproduction was the make-up of the president's hand-picked Council on Bioethics. The president formed this council in 2001, following his executive order opposing embryonic stem cell research, and the revolving door of appointments here seemed only to swing in the direction of the White House. To chair the council, President Bush chose Dr. Leon Kass, a well-respected ethicist and academic who happened to have a point of view that fit conveniently alongside the president's. Dr. Kass believes that all biological research involving human embryos is unethical and against God's will. His position is unwavering on this. At least one independent bioethicist, Arthur Kaplan of the University of Pennsylvania, told the *Washington Post* that Dr. Kass seemed to be pushing for a consensus on the council that would be in line with the White House's preordained views on a topic.

Not only was the chairman's position filled by an individual who shared the anti-scientific views of the Bush administration, but other members of the council were cut from the same cloth. And, when it turned out they weren't, they were removed from the council. Initially, there were two council members who supported progressive research, but in February 2004, presumably with the president's knowledge, Dr. Kass dismissed them. One of the dismissed council members, Dr. Elizabeth Blackburn, a renowned biologist at the University of California at San Francisco, told reporters following her ouster that she believed President Bush was "stacking the council with the compliant."

The other dismissed member was Dr. William May, emeritus professor of ethics at Southern Methodist University, who also made the mistake of not sharing the president's views on stem cell research.

In their place, the president installed three new members—Dr. Benjamin Carson, director of pediatric neurosurgery at Johns Hopkins University; Peter Lawler, professor of government at Georgia's Berry College; and Diana Schaub, chairman of the political science department at Loyola College in Maryland. According to the *Washington Post*, all three had public back-grounds to suggest that the Council on Bioethics might have an easier time reaching a consensus in the future:

- Dr. Carson was a noted motivational speaker who often spoke about religion and the Bible in his talks, once bemoaning the fact that "we live in a nation where we can't talk about God in public."

- Prof. Lawler warned in the *Weekly Standard* that the United States must soon "become clear as a nation that abortion is wrong."

- Prof. Schaub referred to scientific research involving human embryos as "the evil of the willful destruction of human life."

And it was downhill from there. Dr. Kass left the council in 2005 and was replaced by Edmund Pellegrino, a Catholic ethicist and professor emeritus at Georgetown Medical Center, and the former president of Catholic University. Dr. Pellegrino is a founding member of Do No Harm, an organization whose goals include "the development of treatments and therapies that do not require the destruction of human life, including the human embryo."

There seems to be a real anti-women agenda in Washington these days—and as long as religious conservatives have a voice I suspect they'll be using it to sound the alarm on matters of human sexuality and reproduction. I've struggled to understand it and get beyond it, but I'm afraid there's still a general and prevailing squeamishness when it comes to talking about sex. This shared uneasiness seems to get in the way of any kind of healthy debate in this area. Let's face it, a lot of us have a hard time talking to our own children about these issues, and here we are in the U.S. Congress, trying to have a conversation about IUDs and condoms and Depo-Provera injections. It's slow-going. It's awkward. And then on top of that squeamishness we have the many tentacles of the Catholic Church, trying to influence a dialogue that's already difficult to begin with. At the other end, it's like we're walking up a down escalator and getting nowhere.

One of the most alarming examples of this right-wing bewilderment took place on the House floor during a late-night debate in July 1998. We were debating the Appropriations bill, which funds the Federal Employees Health Benefit Plan. Nita Lowey, the ranking Democrat on the subcommittee with jurisdiction over the bill, decided we should require the plans to provide insurance coverage for contraception, just as they do for other prescription drugs. After all, Nita reasoned, the plans covered Viagra. It seemed right and fair that female federal employees should be able to obtain birth control under their insurance. (Some readers whose birth control is covered by their private insurance plans might be surprised to learn that this was not already part of the package of the federal health insurance.)

Nita very sensibly offered her amendment, which said that plans would be required to offer coverage for the five types of contraception already approved by the Food and Drug Administration. She took the additional step of exempting religious plans that, as a matter of conscience, did not cover prescription contraception, fully expecting that this one small concession would anticipate any reasonable objection to her amendment.

Somehow, this small, sensible effort turned into a sideshow on the House floor. Somewhere in the middle of the heated back-

and-forth that attached to Nita's proposal, I caught myself wishing it was taking place in the light of day, so American women could get a real sense of the religious right's congressional agenda—which was not just to ban abortion, apparently, but birth control as well. Instead, the amendment was called up in the middle of the night, when no one was watching, setting in motion one of the most off-the-wall debates I've ever participated in on the House floor. Chris Smith, the self-appointed congressional defender of the right-to-life movement, rose in "very strong" opposition to Nita's amendment. The Pro-Choice Caucus had expected as much, so a sizeable group of mostly female members of Congress had gathered on the floor to support passage of the Lowey amendment and to counter any arguments that came our way.

Representative Smith offered an amendment to Nita's amendment, which said, "Notwithstanding any provision of this act, no funds in this act may be used to require any contract to include a term for coverage of *abortifacients*."

The term *abortifacient* is a favorite term of anti-choice activists, but let's be clear: It is not a medical term; it's not a legal term; you can find it in the Random House dictionary, but that's only because it's seeped into common usage, the way it's bandied about constantly by the right wing. It's really just a coinage of the religious right to refer to any contraceptive device or medication that could be said to discourage or prevent implantation of a fertilized egg in a woman's uterus. (Maybe I'm just naïve, or maybe I missed a meeting, but I thought that was the whole point of contraception, to *discourage* or *prevent* implantation.)

It was understandable, then, that those of us in the Pro-Choice Caucus became a little confused over which contraceptives Representative Smith meant to allow federal employees to receive with their federal health insurance coverage. Part of the reason we were so confused, I think, was because Representative Smith was himself confused—and a little flustered, too. When he rose to debate his amendment, he faced a large group of concerned congresswomen on the other side of the aisle, determined to make him spell out exactly what he intended to allow or disallow. Nita led the charge, with the rest of us standing on the floor behind her, urging her on.

I'll quote at length from the *Congressional Record*, to give the full flavor of the moment:

> **REP. CHRIS SMITH:** Let me make it very clear that part of the problem with the Lowey amendment was that it did not define contraception. Many of us have been concerned that the pro-abortion lobby and the pro-abortion organizations over the years have tried to fudge the line of demarcation between fertilization post- and pre-fertilization. Many of the chemicals, many of the devices that are now employed that are permitted under the Federal Employees Health Benefits Program do indeed result in many abortions, newly created human lives that are not permitted to implant in their mother's womb. In a nutshell, my amendment is designed to clarify that . . .

> **REP. NITA LOWEY:** . . . I rise to engage the gentleman from New Jersey in a colloquy. I would like to ask the gentleman to define further his amendment. Based upon the information that we have, the FDA has approved five methods of contraception. This is the established definition of contraception . . .

REP. SMITH: If the gentlewoman would yield, let me just ask the gentlewoman, because this will help me in responding, her definition of contraception. Is it before fertilization occurs or is it before implantation in the uterus?

REP. LOWEY: I am sorry. Will the gentleman repeat?

REP. SMITH: Part of the problem we have with the gentlewoman's first amendment, as well as the amendment that was offered and just passed, is a definitional one. How do you define contraception? How do you define pregnancy? For some, it is implantation. For some, it is fertilization . . .

REP. LOWEY: Reclaiming my time.

REP. SMITH: Contraception by definition should mean before a new life has come into being. There are many who want to blur that line and say that chemicals affect the implementation or even after that.

At this point, the congresswomen encouraged Nita to ask Representative Smith to run down the list of each FDA-approved method of birth control, and to specify which methods he sought to allow and which he sought to disallow.

REP. LOWEY: If I may reclaim my time, could the gentleman explain whether this includes the pill?

REP. SMITH: This will have to be determined. There is a body of evidence suggesting that IUDs, for example, may have the impact, and many women are unaware of this, may have the impact of preventing implantation. What my amendment says, that is still permissible under Federal Employees Health Benefit Program, but not mandated.

REP. LOWEY: Reclaiming my time, if I might ask the gentleman, I believe in response to my question as to whether the pill would be included, since the pill is one of the five methods of approving contraception from the FDA, you seem to be questioning this and I would ask the gentleman, if you are not sure whether the pill is an established method of contraception, what would the plans determine?

REP. SMITH: Let me just respond that there are several schools of thought as to what the operation is as to what actually occurs.

Here again, it appeared Representative Smith himself was not too sure if birth control pills would be allowed under his amendment, but the group of us thought it was time to move on. I whispered to Nita that she should press our Republican colleague on the IUD.

Continuing . . .

REP. LOWEY: Reclaiming my time, would the gentleman consider the IUD a form of contraception? This is an approved method of contraception. Or would you consider the IUD an abortifacient?

REP. SMITH: Let me make it very clear there has to be a determination made, and maybe it is about time, with all of the resources at our disposal, we really came to a firm conclusion as to how some of these chemicals and how the IUD actually works, because again, even Planned Parenthood and others will say on their web page that one of the consequences of the IUD may indeed be preventative of implantation.

REP. LOWEY: Reclaiming my time, does the gentleman include the diaphragm as a form of contraception?

REP. SMITH: No. As far as I know, that is not included.

REP. LOWEY: It seems to me the gentleman has questions about the pill, questions about the diaphragm, questions about the IUD, and I assume the gentleman has questions about Depo-Provera and Norplant. Let me say this, there are five established methods of contraception. If the gentleman supports the amendment to not cover abortion, then you are saying that contraception cannot be covered. No method of contraception can be covered.

REP. SMITH: Not at all. Right now the HMOs, and all of the health care providers under the Federal Employees Health Benefits Program, if they choose, can provide any of those methods that you mentioned, from IUDs to Depo-Provera. What your amendment, or what the thrust of your original amendment was to force them to do it.

REP. LOWEY: Reclaiming my time, I just want to make it clear to my colleague that the gentleman from New Jersey, it appears to me from your statement, is trying to make every method of contraception an abortifacient, is that correct?

REP. SMITH: Not at all, and that is putting words in my mouth, and I think that is unfortunate.

It sure sounded to us like that's what Representative Smith had just said. His amendment was very specific. It said it would not allow coverage of any form of birth control he considered an abortifacient, and according to his position in this wacky debate he appeared to believe that all forms of contraception were abortifacients.

Lord knows, we certainly didn't want to put words in the congressman's mouth. He seemed to be having enough trouble doing that all on his own.

REP. LOWEY: Mr. Chairman, if I can make it clear, I think it is very important, my colleagues, that we realize what the gentleman is attempting to achieve with this amendment. He is stating that there is no form of contraception that may not be considered an abortifacient and, therefore, the American women have to understand . . .

REP. SMITH: If the gentlewoman will yield, I did not say that at all . . .

REP. LOWEY: No, I will not yield. I will not yield. That the American people who are listening to this debate have to understand that this Congress wants to tell women that all forms of contraception are abortifacients and they cannot be considered. I would like to make that point again. The majority of American women do support the use of contraceptives. These are very personal decisions, we understand that, and each person has to make it for themselves. But the majority of American women understands that. Now, it seems to me from this discussion, that the gentleman from New Jersey is saying to every woman who may take a birth control pill or use another one of the five accepted methods of contraception that they are abortionists.

REP. SMITH: Not at all.

You really do have to picture this scene, because it was almost other-worldly. We were deep into the wee hours of the morning at this point. Over on the Republican side of the chamber, you had Chris Smith, trying to bar the federal government from paying for birth control for federal employees, but doing it through a sneaky, backdoor method because he knew that the vast majority of Americans supported birth control. And then on our side of the chamber there was Nita Lowey, with about a dozen pro-choice congresswomen standing just behind her, cheering her on and whispering in her ear and wondering what small piece of strangeness we had just stumbled upon.

My colleagues and I went around and around on this for the longest time, until finally former Rep. Nancy Johnson (R-Connecticut) weighed in. Nancy, a feisty, pro-choice Republican who was married to a physician, could always be counted on to get to the heart of a situation, and here she had the final word:

REP. JOHNSON: Is there no limit to my colleague's willingness to impose his concept of when life begins on others? Conception is a process. Fertilization of the egg is part of that process. But if that fertilized egg does not get implanted, it does not grow. And so on throughout the course of pregnancy. For those who do not believe that life begins upon fertilization, but believes, in fact, that that fertilized egg has to be implanted, the gentleman is imposing his judgment as to when life begins on that person and, in so doing, denying them what might be the safest means of contraception available to them.

Some women cannot take the pill. It is too disruptive to them. Some women depend on intrauterine devices and other such contraceptives. When we get to the point where we have the courage to do more research in contraception, we will have many other options to offer women so that they can have safe contraception. For us to make the decision that that woman must choose a means of contraception that reflects any one individual's determination as to when in that process of conception life actually begins is a level of intrusion into conscience, into independence, into freedom that, frankly, I have never witnessed. Even the issue of being for or against abortion is a different issue than we debate here tonight. We have never, ever intruded to this depth . . .

The lines are not clear. They are not simple. I would ask my colleague to respect that we are a nation founded on the belief that we should have freedom of conscience and freedom of religion, and this amendment deeply, deeply compromises those liberties.

Representative Smith's amendment was defeated by a recorded vote of 222–198, which was shocking to me. Enraging, too, that such wrong-headedness was only a dozen votes shy of standing as the prevailing view. Consider that almost two hundred members of Congress voted to bar insurance coverage of legal, FDA-approved birth control methods because the religious right now referred to them as *abortifacients*. The deeply troubling suggestion here was that birth control was no different than abortion to a few too many of our colleagues.

I listened to the vote and thought, *Goodness, are we in trouble!* Then I thought, *If the suburban Republican and Independent women of America heard this debate they would never again vote for a candidate without getting an iron-clad guarantee that they would support birth control when they got to Congress.* It seemed to me a sad and telling footnote to the twentieth century—a tumultuous time that had seen an enormous push for progress and change and civil rights and women's rights and was now reduced to such as this—and, as the calendar turned toward the twenty-first century, I worried what this type of thinking might mean for our future.

In the end, Nita's amendment passed, which pleased us greatly, even as we stood aghast that such a non-controversial issue could draw such a significant number of *no* votes, simply because it had to do with birth control.

I'd thought we were past that, after all these years.

Lately, the debate has turned to emergency contraception, the latest battleground for religious conservatives determined to equate abortion with birth control. At the time of our late-night debate, back in 1998, Plan B, a high-dose birth control pill that can prevent pregnancy if taken within seventy-two hours after intercourse, was only available to women with a doctor's prescription. If you think about it, the entire purpose of *emergency* contraception is defeated if a woman has to find a doctor, get a prescription, and have it filled—all within seventy-two hours. That's why, in 2001, the United Kingdom began allowing pharmacies to dispense emergency contraception without a prescription.

In 2003, the Women's Capital Corporation submitted an application to the FDA requesting approval of Plan B for over-the-counter distribution in the United States. The FDA, by its regular process, referred the issue to two outside committees—which after reviewing forty scientific studies of the safeness and efficacy of the drug voted unanimously that Plan B was safe for nonprescription use and voted 23–4 to recommend switching the drug to over-the-counter status.

Despite this recommendation, in May 2004, the FDA for the first time in its history rejected the recommendation of its scientific panels and issued a "not approved" letter. Acting FDA commissioner Lester Crawford appeared before an Appropriations Committee panel and explained his rationale: "We don't always follow the recommendations of advisory committees," he cautioned. "Advisory committees are generally scientific and medical experts. We have to take what they say and fold it into intelligent and public health policy that protects the American people maximally."

The decision to deny over-the-counter status, even temporarily, to a drug that was considered medically safe and effective—a drug that had been endorsed by the medical community and approved in thirty-three countries—was clearly not based on science, and clearly not in the best interest of American women.

So clearly political was the decision that Susan Wood, the director of the FDA Office of Women's Health, resigned in protest. A group of members of Congress asked the U.S. Government Accountability Office (GAO) to investigate why the recommendations had been rejected. The GAO reported that the process was "unusual" and noted that the decision not to approve the drug may have been made long before the scientific reviews were completed.

Ultimately, the FDA came down in favor of approving Plan B but said that it would not make the pills available without a prescription until the manufacturer could outline a plan to keep the medication from teenagers aged sixteen and younger, or could demonstrate that this group could understand directions for the drug's proper use. Such undue restrictions were not based on any medical evidence to suggest that teenagers were somehow incapable of following a simple set of directions. It was purely a moral decision, based on the morality of a powerful few and forced upon the rest of us with the weight of law.

I heard that and thought, *Gee, if this is what acting commissioner Crawford had in mind when he talked about "protecting the American people maximally," then we're all in trouble.*

Of course, the obstinacy of religious conservatives on matters of birth control doesn't end here, and I'll conclude this chapter with one final (and appalling!) illustration. Even though Plan B was approved for over-the-counter distribution, the administration has steadfastly refused to provide the contraceptive in government settings. I noted earlier that Plan B is not included in the drug formulary on the front lines for our troops, but unbelievably it's also not included in the Department of Justice's protocol for medical and forensic examinations following sexual assault. This oversight is shocking to me, and galling, because it means that the DOJ is not instructing police departments and emergency room personnel to inform women who have just been raped that they could take Plan B birth control within seventy-two hours and avoid becoming pregnant by their attacker.

I joined with eighty-eight colleagues in a bi-partisan letter to Diane M. Stuart, director of the DOJ Office on Violence against Women, to express our outrage. "Women who have been sexually assaulted have a compelling need for quick access to emergency contraception," we wrote. "To be effective, EC must be administered within 72-120 hours of unprotected intercourse, but experts agree that it is more effective the sooner it is taken, making timely access to EC critical . . . Additionally, many hospitals around the country do not have clear protocols on the treatment of sexual assault patients, thereby heightening the need for this national protocol."

Predictably, we received no response to this letter, and as of this writing information about emergency contraception has not been included in the national protocol—which was not surprising. Make no mistake: It's upsetting; it's aggravating; it's maddening, even. But I'm afraid we shot past surprising nearly eight years ago.

TWELVE

"THROUGH NO FAULT ON ANYBODY'S PART"

In my time in the State House and on Capitol Hill, I have been endlessly amazed at some of the policies and positions of my colleagues on the politically charged issue of abortion. Some of the public discourse on abortion is so irrational and mind boggling it leaves me to wonder what the religious right has up its collective sleeve—or, more to the point, what they've slipped into the Kool-Aid.

It's not just irrational; it's irresponsible. It's also irritating, the way the issue seems to infect almost every political action or inaction undertaken by the Bush White House. Incredibly, it reaches all the way to the Middle East, about as far from American soil as one can imagine—at least according to a report in the *Washington Post* that the Bush administration was asking Iraqi occupation authority applicants their views on *Roe v. Wade,* as if their stance on abortion might impact their ability to lead a U.S.-backed government in that region.

If you think it's hard for politicians to talk about widely accepted issues like stem cell research and birth control, imagine how uneasy they become when the topic turns to abortion. Last I heard, abortion is still legal in this country—more than 1.2 million American women chose to have one in 2005, the last year for which statistics are available. The majority of Americans support a woman's right to make such a choice; yet one of the most frustrating battles we have in Congress is the ongoing effort to advance commonsense policies surrounding abortion and to put down all the nonsense arguments lobbed by religious conservatives intended to undercut a woman's right to choose.

To be sure, all pro-choice members of Congress support the constitutional right to abortion, but we also try to create policies that make abortion safe, legal, and rare. And yet every so often we must stand on the side of reason and fight the good fight, because it's ever-important to protect a woman's right to choose.

Consider the Sisyphean example of my friend and colleague Susan Davis (D-California). Every year, on the Military Appropriations bill, Susan offers the same amendment allowing American servicewomen to receive abortions at U.S. military hospitals using their own money. It's a commonsense, practical response to a real problem, and for the life of me I can't understand how anyone could object to it. Susan can't either, which I guess is why she valiantly offers it each year.

Unfortunately, Susan's effort runs counter to the infamous Hyde Amendment, which has been the law of the land since 1976. The Hyde Amendment stipulates that no abortions can be funded with federal dollars. However, the problem with a blanket application of the Hyde Amendment to every federal dollar spent, directly or indirectly, is that it often leads to appalling circumstances.

Think about it: What happens to one of our servicewomen if she has an unplanned pregnancy while stationed overseas, in someplace like Baghdad or Kabul? It doesn't happen often, thank God, but it happens. There's no place for her to go to receive a medically safe abortion, and because of the federal restrictions on abortion she can't get one in one of our own military hospitals.

This means she has to arrange for an extended leave to Germany or some other developed nation and seek treatment there, all at her own expense. It's a shame and an indignation—that women who are serving our country should have to chase treatment like that. The Davis amendment does not require our medical personnel to perform the procedure against their will, and it still requires the servicewomen to pay for the abortion but does allow the procedure to take place in military hospitals—a small fairness, wouldn't you agree?

But a small fairness only goes so far in the debate on abortion, without common sense to push things along. Every year, Susan gets around two hundred votes for her amendment but ultimately falls short, and it's always a heartbreaking defeat. She talks about servicewomen who can't even arrange for a medical leave until their second trimester—which, if you're morally opposed to abortion in the first place is even more objectionable, in addition to presenting greater medical risks. And the debate has grown even more heartbreaking since the Afghan and Iraqi wars. Here we are, putting women into harm's way every day, and we won't even bend our no-funding policy even a little.

For several years in the late 1990s, I offered an amendment of my own, trying to fix a situation that was doubly difficult because it involved both abortion *and* federal prisoners. Here again, I thought it was a practical, commonsense response to a fundamental problem—namely, to allow federal funds to be used for abortion services for women in prison. Let's say a female inmate was raped by a guard, which unfortunately does happen. Let's say that act of violence resulted in a pregnancy. What's that female inmate expected to do? She doesn't have any money. If she works in prison, she earns anywhere between 12 cents and $1.15 per hour. Even if she earns at the maximum rate and manages to save all of her money, she would not be able to afford an abortion within the first trimester, and at that point we'd be facing some of the same complications we talked about regarding later-term abortions for our military women. And if the pregnant inmate carries the baby to term, what happens then? What happens to the baby?

On a cost basis alone, it's probably cheaper for the government to pay for an abortion, if indeed that was the woman's choice, than to spring for appropriate prenatal and postnatal care, and the cost of associated child services. It's logical. It's humane. It's just.

And yet we always got far fewer votes for this amendment than Susan got for hers, I'm sorry to report. Our high-water mark was 169 votes, which wasn't exactly an overwhelming show of support. My colleagues just couldn't get past the fact that I was seeking federal funding for *any* abortions, under *any* circumstances, even if it made economic and logistical sense. At some point, I finally stopped offering the amendment. Many people told me they just didn't want to deal with it any more, but I'm hoping that under the next administration common sense will be restored and we can allow this one exception to the Hyde Amendment.

To tell you the truth, I just don't get what the religious right is thinking. Instead of supporting comprehensive sex education and birth control to reduce the number of unwanted pregnancies and abortions, conservative Republicans have tried to scare American women into believing that abortions carry all sorts of mental and physical health risks. In this way, they hope to dissuade women from having abortions. It's like they've taken a page out of Tom Coburn's playbook, seeking to put "black box" labels on condoms to persuade teens that abstinence is the only way to prevent unwanted pregnancy or STDs.

Here's just one example of how the religious right's extreme agenda can get in the way of a reasonable discussion on abortion or birth control—a discussion, by the way, that wasn't meant to be about abortion or birth control when it started out. There has been an ongoing effort in the Energy and Commerce Committee to expand funding and research into post-partum depression, a genuine medical condition suffered by many women after the birth of a child. Unfortunately, the right wing insists on conflating this issue with the question of whether abortions cause a condition called *post-abortion syndrome*. Now, post-abortion syndrome is not a condition recognized by the medical community, but the religious right continues to argue that it affects a large number of women who have had abortions.

This is a familiar tactic of the religious conservatives—to concoct a willful distortion and present it as fact. Once again, the thinking here was that if you can't overturn *Roe v. Wade* and take legalized abortion off the books, you might as well at least try to keep women from considering abortion as a viable option. One way to do this is to introduce the notion that an abortion carries serious emotional consequences, whether or not there is research or evidence to support such a claim.

Obviously, the decision to seek an abortion is a difficult and painful one for any pregnant woman, and I don't mean to diminish the real anguish that some women experience in choosing this option. But the relentless effort by the religious right to assign a clinical diagnosis of depression to women recovering from an abortion, and to equate a fabricated condition with the documented diagnosis of post-partum depression was irresponsible at best, and unconscionable at worst.

For the last four sessions of Congress, Joe Pitts (R-Pennsylvania) has introduced legislation that would require federal funds to be spent to research so-called post-abortion syndrome, and to provide services to patients suffering from the condition. However, the established medical community has researched the claims concerning post-abortion syndrome but found no basis for them. In 1989, the American Psychological Association (APA) assembled a panel of experts to review evidence of the psychological risks of abortion. The panel unanimously concluded that legal abortion, "does not create psychological hazards for most women undergoing the procedure." That view has not changed in the last twenty years.

In contrast, post-partum depression *is* a genuine medical condition suffered by many women. My colleague Bobby Rush (D-Illinois) has fought for years for legislation to study and treat this condition, only to have the right wing repeatedly muck up his efforts with its made-up condition.

At a hearing in 2004, the Republican committee chairman scheduled testimony on Bobby's bill, including a heart-rending account by a woman named Carol Blocker, whose daughter Melanie had committed suicide as the result of untreated post-partum depression. It was a powerful appeal. The chairman also scheduled testimony from Michaelene Fredenburg, president of Life Resource Network, to talk about post-abortion syndrome—and it was almost insulting to have to consider her remarks alongside those of a woman who'd lost her daughter.

Perhaps the most compelling witness on the panel that day was Dr. Nada Stotland, professor of psychiatry and obstetrics and gynecology at Rush Medical College in Chicago, who spoke on behalf of the APA. I'll quote from Dr. Stotland's testimony at length, because her comments stand in eloquent support of my position:

We tend to use psychiatric terms such as depression and psychosis imprecisely, so let me briefly discuss these illnesses in the context of the Diagnostic and Statistical Manual of Mental Disorders, the internationally recognized standard for the diagnosis of mental disorders. Depression is classified in DSM by severity, recurrence and association with mania. Major depression is a serious illness, typified by a depressed mood most of the day, nearly every day, for at least two weeks, markedly diminished interest or pleasure in nearly all activities, weight loss or increased appetite, insomnia or hypersomnia, fatigue and recurrent thoughts of death or suicide.

Psychosis is part of a severe mental disorder and is characterized by a person's gross impairment in perceiving reality. A psychotic person may be delusional, or may experience hallucinations, disorganized speech, or disorganized or catatonic behavior.

With those definitions in mind, I'd like to say a quick word about post-partum disorders before discussing "so-called post-abortion depression and psychosis."

Today we know that disturbances can occur in the post-partum period in the form of transeunt baby blues, or much more seriously as Post-Partum Depression and Psychosis. As you have heard today, left undiagnosed or untreated, the consequences of Post-Partum Psychosis can be horrific. We need more attention to these illnesses, particularly in populations that traditionally have restricted access to health and mental health care. So-called "post-abortion depression and psychosis" are, however, created designations by those who believe that abortions can have a long-term impact on the mental health of humans who elect to terminate a pregnancy.

In fact, data clearly shows that the vast majority of women have abortions without psychiatric sequelae. Even C. Everett Koop, M.D., who was President Reagan's Surgeon General and was personally very much opposed to abortion, found that, "The psychological effects of abortion are miniscule from a public health perspective." This is clear. Abortions are not a significant cause of mental illness. The psychological outcome of abortion is optimized when women are able to make decisions on the basis of their own values, beliefs and circumstances, free from pressure or coercion, and to have those decisions supported by their families, friends and society in general. This is not to say that there aren't any women who feel deeply distressed about having abortions, but it does not follow that there is a causal link between abortion and severe mental or physical illness. Self-selected accounts of post-abortion distress, however personally compelling, are not scientific studies.

As my colleague (and now U.S. Senator) Sherrod Brown said in his opening remarks, the Republicans' plan to once again link post-abortion syndrome with the subject under review was once again inappropriate. What should have been a non-partisan, science-based discussion on clinical instances of depression following pregnancy was now just another Republican attempt to politicize the issue and discourage American women from exercising their right to choose. "I'm sorry that one of our witnesses has dealt with depression that she attributes to the circumstances surrounding her abortion," noted Sherrod, the ranking Democrat on the Subcommittee on Health. "I'm not surprised, though, that the majority chose to introduce the topic of abortion in this debate. Had the majority been truly interested in expanding the focus of this hearing to look at the mental health of women who have been pregnant, then where are the witnesses who have experienced miscarriage, or stillbirth, or adoption for that matter? Where is the witness who is currently facing an unintended pregnancy who didn't know about birth control because her high school couldn't get funding for comprehensive sex education?

"Anti-choice members of Congress have every right to promote their agenda, but it's a shame they chose to turn this important public health hearing into yet another attack on the reproductive rights of women. This hearing should promote the well-being of women, not compromise it. Post-partum depression is a serious mental health threat. Its impact on women and families is enormous. We should keep our eye on the ball."

Yes, we certainly should—but try telling that to the Republican members of our subcommittee who kept trotting out witnesses offering first-hand tales of post-abortion woe and distress as if the very future of choice in America depended on it.

In 2007, after the Democrats took control of Congress, the new Health Committee Chairman Frank Pallone (D-New Jersey) scheduled another hearing on Bobby Rush's post-partum depression bill. All the witnesses from the 2004 hearing were invited back, and they were now joined by Mary Jo Codey, former first lady of New Jersey, herself a survivor of post-partum depression.

It was the same story all over again, as my conservative colleagues doggedly injected their discussion of post-abortion syndrome into the mix—and, in a misguided attempt to examine these issues, Rep. Nathan Deal (R-Georgia) stepped into big-time trouble, at least with me, and gave us all a glimpse into his real thinking on abortion.

In his opening remarks, Representative Deal said, "I hope as we go through this hearing and subsequent legislation itself that we can begin to advance the cause of understanding and dealing with a very serious issue that confronts every woman with the birth of a child, or as we will learn, I'm sure, a woman who suffers an abortion or perhaps even just an involuntary termination of a pregnancy through no fault on anybody's part."

Implicit in Rep. Deal's remarks was the suggestion that if a woman seeks an abortion, she is somehow at fault; if she has a miscarriage, the pregnancy will have been terminated "through no fault on anybody's part." The implication was deeply offensive to me and to the other pro-choice members of the committee—as I'm sure they would have been to the majority of American women if they'd had the opportunity to consider them.

The distinction, in the not-so-subtle manner of Christian conservatives out to browbeat the rest of us into seeing the world through their distorted lens, was everything.

As luck would have it, I was scheduled to follow Representative Deal to make my own opening statement. I was so outraged by his comments that I could not let them stand, so here's what I said: "The effects of post-partum depression can be quite devastating. I look forward to hearing the testimony from our panel here today about ways that we can explore treatments and research for this condition and about how [this] bill can expedite the process . . . And the debate is characterized by things that my good friend and respected colleague, Mr. Deal, just talked about, where he said even pregnancies that are terminated at 'no fault of the woman.' That is offensive to women throughout this country and it has no place in a legitimate debate like the discussion we're going to have today on post-partum depression."

I was so angry over this, I thought I'd turn red. It was bad enough that the religious right kept confusing science with religion, even on issues relating to a non-partisan medical condition like post-partum depression, and yet I simply couldn't get past the fact that a member of Congress would make the odious claim that if a woman miscarried it was no fault of her own, but if she had an abortion there was fault to be assigned.

At some point, the committee hearing broke so we could go to the floor to vote. Representative Deal sought me out on the way over. He could tell I was mad, so he asked me what was wrong. I reminded him what he'd said, and explained how it was insulting to women on both sides of the abortion argument. He thought about it, and he apologized, and that was that. His apology was sincere, I believed, but it didn't change the fact that this was how he thought. No, he hadn't set out to set me off. No, he wasn't just shooting off his mouth to rile me and the other pro-choice women in the room. Deep down, he really believed that abortion was the fault of the woman, and that's what bubbled forth when he spoke.

That particular hearing was also illustrative in the way the Republicans attempted to insert their own agenda into the proceedings—a sleight of hand that did not go unnoticed, and one that would become emblematic of the persistent efforts of the majority party to undermine a woman's right to choose. Remember, this was a hearing on post-partum depression, and yet at every opportunity the Bush conservatives sought to include discussion of a phenomenon they insisted on calling *post-abortion syndrome*—a "condition" that has not been recognized or even seriously considered by the APA.

A similar misinformation campaign was taken up by the religious right in an attempt to convince women that abortions caused an increase in the risk of breast cancer. For the longest time, this had been one of the principal claims of the right wing in its warning to women that abortion was dangerous. However, there was and there remains no evidence to support the claim; in fact, the research clearly demonstrates that there is no statistical difference in cases of breast cancer between women who have had abortions and women who have not had abortions.

For a time in the late 1990s, the following statement was clearly displayed on the National Cancer Institute's website, which was administered by the National Institutes of Health, a federal agency: "The current body of scientific evidence suggests that women who have had either induced or spontaneous abortions have the same risk as other women for developing breast cancer."

End of story? Not so fast. Jump ahead to 2001, shortly after President Bush assumed office, when the information on the website was changed to the following: "The possible relationship between abortion and breast cancer has been examined in over thirty published studies since 1957. Some studies have reported statistically significant evidence of an increased risk of breast cancer in women who have had abortions, while others have merely suggested an increased risk. Other studies have found no increase in risk among women who have had an interrupted pregnancy."

Where there was once scientific and statistical certainty there was now considerable room for doubt, according to the same federal agency—even though there had been no new studies and no new information in this area between the time of the original NCI posting and the revised posting. The only change, really, was the shift from the Clinton administration to the Bush administration, and somewhere in the reshuffling the state of the science was being thrown into question because it no longer served the purpose of the right wing.

Finally, in February 2003, with controversy still swirling around the issue, the National Cancer Institute convened a workshop to review all existing studies on the relationship between pregnancy and breast cancer. The conclusion? Having an abortion or a miscarriage does not increase the risk of breast cancer.

I heard that and thought, *Hmmm, I wonder what the NCI will say now on its website?*

THIRTEEN

A FOOLISH CONSISTENCY

For a while, the Bush administration was to be applauded for taking on the global fight against HIV/AIDS with its 2002 proposal to spend $15 billion on AIDS prevention and treatment efforts in Africa and the Caribbean over the next five years. It was one of the few Republican initiatives I could wholeheartedly endorse on this president's watch, but then the right wing inserted itself into this all-important effort and gummed up the works.

Once again, we might have known—only here the gumming up was truly astonishing for the way religious conservatives sought to export their ideologically based abstinence-only policies on wildly diverse cultures that didn't necessarily buy into prevailing American views regarding faith and family. And yet the intransigence of the Bush White House is such that it seeks to impose the president's social and religious views on the rest of the world and fully expects the rest of the world to fall in line right alongside. Abstinence-only doesn't work here in the United States, and yet the administration has been determined to foist it on other countries where sexual mores are far different than they are here. The actions of the Republican majority during the first six years of the Bush administration seemed to suggest the view that it's our money and we can do whatever we want with it—including taking the pompous position that those we mean to help with our humanitarian aid must believe in the same God, follow the same customs, and uphold the same principles.

A carefully conceived program of global HIV/AIDS awareness and prevention could have accomplished a great deal with
that kind of funding; after all, $15 billion is a huge number in fed-
eral budget terms. Instead, our ill-conceived program has merely
wasted a lot of money and infuriated a lot of people. Consider the
inroads that had been made in this area in the country of Uganda,
before the Bush-backed doctrine of intolerance and abstinence
set things back. What worked in Uganda, beginning in the early
1990s, was a comprehensive approach to sex education and HIV/
AIDS awareness, known in international relief circles as the *ABC*
approach—A, for encouraging Abstinence; B, for Being faithful;
and C, for using Condoms. Statistics showed that by attempting
to change the behavior of young Ugandans in all three areas, the
spread of HIV in that country was slowed dramatically.

Indeed, our Subcommittee on Health heard moving testimony from a native Ugandan, Sophia Mukasa Monico, director of AIDS programming for the Global Health Council, at a
hearing on the global health pandemic in March 2003. "I cannot
stress strongly enough that all these program elements need to
be in place for prevention to work," said Ms. Monico, who had
previously worked as executive director of the AIDS Support
Organization, widely recognized as an innovator in the field of
AIDS care and support. "As a Ugandan, I am deeply concerned
when I hear people talking about a single element of our successful national program—for example, abstinence—which is always
out of context, and ascribe all of our achievements to that one
element. They all must be implemented together in order for prevention to work."

Clearly, the spread of HIV/AIDS was and remains an epidemic of catastrophic proportions. In the previous two decades,

the virus had become an international public health crisis, with far-reaching implications to our global economy and our wellspring of humanity. As of 2003, more than 22 million people worldwide had died of AIDS, while more than 60 million people had been infected with HIV. It was projected at that time that 200 million people would become infected with the virus in the next fifteen years. HIV/AIDS was the leading cause of death in sub-Saharan Africa, and the fourth-leading cause of death around the world. And underneath these troubling numbers was an even more troubling subset of numbers: in 2002 alone, more than 600,000 children under fifteen years of age had died of AIDS, the great majority of them having been infected at birth, while another 800,000 children had been newly infected in just the previous year.

Also clearly, this homegrown Ugandan solution to its own AIDS epidemic emerged as a kind of beacon of hope, as concern over the health crisis deepened in the United States and abroad. Critics of the ABC approach in African nations like Uganda argued that the social mores of the country would work against such an effort, since most African women did not have a strong voice in matters of sexual negotiation and since African men were not inclined toward monogamy. However, beginning in 1989, Uganda started to integrate HIV awareness into its schools, and to adapt behavior-changing messages into its curriculum. They called their approach *life skills education,* believing that a curriculum based only on abstinence would not offer a practical foundation for its students. And, for the first time, the education effort targeted boys as well as girls and encouraged them to be a part of the solution. The result? Between 1989 and 1995, just a few years into the full-scale launch of the ABC program, casual sexual encounters in Uganda had fallen by over 50 percent. Further, an overwhelming majority of Ugandan women (98.5 percent) reported that they had either been abstinent or faithful to their regular partners in the period of time under review. Faithfulness among African women had never been a serious problem, especially as it related to the relative unfaithfulness of African men, but this was a tremendous show of fidelity just the same. And further still, in an international Demographic and Health survey, Ugandan women ranked first among all African women in their perceived ability to refuse unwanted or unprotected sex.

Whatever they were doing, it was working, and soon even ABC's critics took note. The Ugandan program stood as an effective model, and it wasn't long before other nations followed suit. For a fleeting moment it seemed we might finally be making some headway in this area—and that's about the time the Bush proposal surfaced with the promise of all that American aid to underwrite these programs. But the money was ideologically encumbered, meant to reinforce a narrow world view.

In addition to merely underwriting these programs we sought to undermine them as well. Under the Bush initiative, the bulk of U.S. aid was distributed through religious organizations specializing in relief efforts in sub-Saharan Africa and throughout the Caribbean. Invariably, these faith-based organizations did not believe in birth control. They would teach A and B, abstinence and being faithful, while the question of C—where to go to receive condoms, and how to use them effectively—was always referred to another organization, which typically meant it would go unanswered. In this way, of course, the matter of birth control was essentially ignored, in much the same way it was ignored at home.

"Bush's Paleolithic obscurantism about the condom is nothing new," wrote Doug Ireland in *The Nation*. "The Bush Administration has weakened the global effort to fight AIDS, particularly in those developing countries whose governments have only just begun to come to grips with combating the epidemic through scientifically proven means like the condom. . ."

And it wasn't just the United States' ability to withhold funding to programs that continued to promote condom use, or to target only faith-based distribution networks that supported its abstinence-only message. No, the far right sought to advance its agenda in other ways as well. In December 2002, to cite just one not-so-subtle example, the U.S. delegation at the United Nations–sponsored Asian and Pacific Population Conference attempted to delete the phrase "consistent condom use" from a list of acceptable methods for preventing HIV infection.

Over time, the net effect of these contrary efforts damaged the good work that was already underway. All of a sudden, the success rate of some of these homegrown programs began to dip, and international human rights organizations expressed concern. Condom use is central to our ability to fight the spread of HIV/AIDS around the world. In addition to the ABC effort in Uganda, there have also been successful awareness initiatives promoting effective condom use in such diverse countries as Cambodia, Senegal, Thailand, and the Dominican Republic. In many of these countries, incidence of infidelity is fairly common among males, but, with regular and proper condom use, at least those men who continue to have sex outside of marriage do not infect their wives or their children. And so, absolutely, the condom is a key component of any practical strategy to fight HIV/AIDS.

A group of us in Congress became so incensed at the president's apparent misuse of U.S. funds and authority in this regard that we wrote yet another letter to HHS Secretary Tommy Thompson. A similar group had written similar letters to Secretary Thompson over the years, criticizing various gaps in the public health policies of the Bush White House. Secretary Thompson is a decent and thoughtful man, and I guess we kept writing because we thought someday we might receive a thoughtful response, or at least shore him up in making his case to the president.

We wrote:

> *Despite the overwhelming evidence that comprehensive HIV prevention can save millions of lives, the Bush administration has persisted in its efforts to undermine support for effective programs at every level. The administration has used numerous means to undermine public confidence in condoms as an effective barrier to HIV infection, has erroneously attributed declines in HIV prevalence in countries such as Uganda solely to abstinence, and has reduced funding overall to the primary health care programs on which effective prevention strategies must be built . . .*
>
> *Undermining effective HIV/AIDS prevention in the United States in pursuit of an unproven ideological goal is dangerous enough . . . but impeding international HIV/AIDS prevention efforts on ideological grounds could be catastrophic. The combined effects of these actions is to reduce the use of condoms and impede the practice of safer sex. These efforts could result in hundreds of thousands of new infections and unnecessary deaths from HIV/AIDS around the world. At a time when 15,000 people are newly infected with HIV* every day, *there can be no justification for pursuing anything other than comprehensive, evidence-based programs employing all available prevention measures.*

Sadly, there was no response. Again.

In 2006, the Government Accountability Office released an eighty-seven page report lambasting Bush's global HIV/AIDS effort. One of the chief criticisms of the GAO report was that the Office of the U.S. Global AIDS Coordinator, which oversaw the distribution of program funds, was required to allocate two-thirds of its spending on programs promoting abstinence, while spending on programs to reduce or prevent mother-to-child transmission of the virus was cut in order to meet those abstinence spending targets.

Another absurd international initiative that just keeps sticking to us like a bad suit is the U.S. policy on international contraception. We can trace this policy to a global "gag rule" on international family planning money first imposed by the Reagan administration. The gag rule, also known as the Mexico City policy, prohibits the U.S. Agency for International Development (USAID) from granting family-planning funds to any overseas health center unless it agrees not to use its own money for abortion services, advocacy, or abortion counseling or referrals. In other words, if an overseas agency uses its own funds for anything relating to abortion, it is not eligible to receive any grants or aid from the United States.

Remember, the United States has had a policy against federally funded abortions abroad since 1973, when Sen. Jesse Helms (R-South Carolina) passed an amendment to the Foreign Operations Appropriations bill. The Mexico City policy goes much, much further, because it bans family planning money from organizations that use *their own funds* for these activities. The thinking behind this sinister policy is an unfounded fear that international agencies might take federal dollars and use them for birth control so they can shift their own money toward abortions. It's an argument of fungibility.

Predictably, this policy has not stopped or slowed the rate of abortions around the world: the respected British medical journal *The Lancet* recently reported that the international rate of abortion has remained steady in countries where abortion is both legal and illegal. Instead, the policy has restricted the availability of birth control. In fact, since 2001, the United States has stopped shipping contraceptives to twenty developing countries in Africa, Asia, and the Middle East.

Here again, the United States has re-imagined its policy against federally funded abortions, at home and abroad, to somehow restrict the flow of family planning resources to those most in need.

The Mexico City policy lasted throughout the Reagan and George H.W. Bush administrations and was repealed by executive order when President Clinton took office in 1993. However, each year thereafter, anti-choice activists in Congress tried to restore the rule, and in 1999 they finally hit upon a silver bullet. They linked the Mexico City language to payment of the United States' back dues to the United Nations language. For some years, for a variety of reasons, the United States had refused to pay its back dues to the United Nations. The tab was now close to $1 billion. The failure had become an international embarrassment, and the Clinton administration and Democrats in Congress were eager to fix the problem. And so, once again, the global gag rule was in effect.

After the 2000 election, as you might suspect, the matter worsened. As one of his first acts as president, George W. Bush reinstituted the Mexico City language. In 2003, he expanded the policy to cover the entire State Department budget. Every year, we tried to reverse this draconian policy when we considered the Foreign Operations spending bill, with varying degrees of success. Some years we were able to pass language through the Senate effectively repealing the Mexico City policy, but that language would somehow never appear in the final bill and the monies were denied year after year.

I'm tired of being embarrassed by U.S. policy in this area. Giving poor women around the world control over the size of their families is one of the most important things we can do. First and foremost, it's the right thing to do, plain and simple. For hundreds of millions of impoverished, uneducated women, family planning could mean the difference between starvation and a subsistence lifestyle. It's also environmentally sound. Controlling the size of families ultimately controls the use of resources. This means less devastation of rainforests and other eco-systems and better public health in developing countries. This is one of the reasons such a diverse coalition of groups has come together to support robust international family planning programs—not just groups like Planned Parenthood, but organizations like the Alliance for Justice, which opposes the restrictions on free speech that the Mexico City language imposes, and the Sierra Club.

When the Democrats regained control of Congress in 2006, one of our top agenda items was to reverse this terrible policy. After the new Congress convened, one of the first initiatives Louise Slaughter and I undertook as co-chairs of the Pro-Choice Caucus was to meet with leaders of the choice groups and embark on a more pro-active strategy. In years past, we were just playing defense, but now we were in a position to take positive action. We decided collectively that our top two priorities would be the repeal of the Mexico City policy and the elimination of federal money for abstinence-only sex education.

As noted earlier, we haven't been able to eliminate money for abstinence-only sex education—and, unfortunately, we hit a brick wall at 1600 Pennsylvania Avenue on the Mexico City policy as well. My colleague Nita Lowey has spent a great deal of time on this issue, and she decided that we should call the anti-choice members' bluff. Rather than repeal the entire Mexico City policy, she suggested, we should just *partially* repeal it. We would add language in the Foreign Operations bill stipulating that health centers otherwise ineligible for USAID assistance could receive U.S.-donated condoms and contraceptives. We thought, *How could people object to the donation of actual birth control devices? How could such a program be tied in any way to abortion? How could it even be suggested that it was abortion-related?* But of course the right wing *did* object. Religious conservatives *did* manage to draw a line from this practical proposal to distribute condoms and contraceptives to the ever-looming issue of choice, and we were reminded yet again that the real objection of these anti-choice groups is to birth control *and* abortion, taken together. They just don't like to come right out and say it because they know most of their constituents support the use of birth control.

Nita was able to get her language included in the bill that came to the House floor in June 2007—but sure enough, Rep. Chris Smith raised his conservative voice yet again and offered an amendment to strip the birth control distribution language. Still, we pressed on. Our Pro-Choice Caucus whipped the vote, and we were somewhat gratified to win. The reason I offer the qualifier *somewhat* is, like on other birth control issues, we barely won the vote, by a margin of 218–205. Even after the Democratic takeover of Congress, we had only twelve Republicans vote *no* with us, while twenty-five Democrats voted *yes*.

But a win was a win and our language was in the bill, which went over to the Senate for consideration. The Senate, which has always been more supportive of international family planning funding, voted to repeal the global gag rule in its entirety. Sadly, despite modification by both Houses, President Bush threatened to veto the legislation if it came to his desk containing language allowing for birth control. The Democratic leadership decided to save the fight for another day and stripped our language from the Omnibus Appropriations bill sent to President Bush in December 2007.

So now here we are, all these years after our first awareness and prevention efforts, and the spread of HIV/AIDS continues to loom as the leading threat to our global health. In family planning, the president has made denial of condoms and other widely used and widely approved birth control devices to millions of people around the world one of his top priorities. He continues to allow discussions on AIDS prevention and global family planning to become permeated with talk of religion over science—and in this way continues to stand against the majority of Americans. In June 2007, Planned Parenthood released a poll reporting that 75 percent of all voters and 82 percent of voters conflicted by the issue of abortion were strongly in favor of Congress passing laws protecting the rights of individuals to access contraception. That's an overwhelming tally, and I have to believe the president and his supporters are merely counting on our preoccupation with other matters to allow them to pursue their own course on this issue.

Most Americans are in agreement, and they stand in utter disbelief at these policies—while I stand ashamed that despite my best efforts and the best efforts of my rational colleagues, our nation continues to get in the way of progressive science and progressive education and progressive health care, instead of standing out in front.

It's time once again to restate the obvious: the only moral, ethical, and scientifically valid approach to HIV prevention is a comprehensive approach. Should abstinence be a part of that? Absolutely, but only a part. We need to arm individuals in these at-risk societies with information and skills to practice abstinence, monogamy, *and* safer sex. Alongside this effort, we need to make birth control available to the world community where it is sorely needed to help curb the global population crisis and to ease poverty.

And we need to do so immediately.

CLOSING ARGUMENTS

As I hope to have shown, the political malpractice of religious conservatives in Congress and among members of the Bush administration has been malignant, self-serving, and unconscionable. Because of the power of the religious right, I'm afraid the defeat of the Republican majority in Congress will not erase the stain of the persistent efforts to undermine scientific progress in the name of God any time soon.

I hope, too, that readers of this text will be as shocked to read of some of the antics of their elected officials and their president as I have been to experience most of them first-hand.

So what are we to make of this mess? Hard to say. I believe we are at a crisis point when it comes to the legislation of matters relating even peripherally to human sexuality and reproduction. Because of the undue influence of a small group of vocal and prominent religious fanatics, as well as the unwillingness to oppose this phenomenon or even to talk about it broadly, our public policy surrounding the issues of sex and science has suffered.

This lapse has very real consequences in the lives of Americans and in the lives of human beings around the world.

Consider:

• last year, for the first time in decades, the rate of teen pregnancy in the United States did not decrease;

- Congress continues to fund abstinence-only sex education programs at the same level, despite their proven ineffectiveness and irrelevance, and despite the fact that an increasing number of states are opting out of the funding;

- the amount of money spent on federally approved embryonic stem cell research has remained low, despite breakthroughs by international and privately funded scientists in both the embryonic stem cell arena and other avenues;

- the United States still has no over-arching ethical oversight of cell-based research occurring in private hands or by the states;

- and, because of the objections of the religious right, the United States has not banned human reproductive cloning, primarily because our sane, science-based legislators will not also ban another progressive technique that uses some of the same technology and shares some of the same nomenclature but offers no insurmountable threat to ethicists.

We need to restore sanity to our public process, and happily there are proposals in Congress that would do just that. For example, some years ago, the Pro-Choice Caucus, working in consultation with allies in the advocacy community such as Planned Parenthood, realized that we weren't communicating the message to our constituents that abortion should never be the first resort. To the contrary, we believe the government should do everything in its power to prevent unwanted pregnancies. To that end, Louise Slaughter and I have developed a comprehensive pregnancy-prevention bill entitled "Prevention First." The

Prevention First bill, which we've drafted with the help of our pro-choice colleagues, seeks to:

- strengthen Medicaid coverage of family planning services;

- end insurance discrimination against women by private health plans to cover FDA-approved prescription contraceptives and related medical services *to the same extent* that they cover prescription drugs and other outpatient medical services;

- improve awareness about emergency contraception;

- provide funding for grants to public and private entities to establish or promote teen pregnancy prevention programs, and for comprehensive sexuality education;

- ensure that information provided about the use of contraception as part of any federally funded sex education, family life education, abstinence education, comprehensive health education, or character education is medically accurate and includes the health benefits and failure rates of such use.

Some of our colleagues are working on complementary pregnancy prevention efforts, like Rep. Rosa DeLauro. Even some of our Democratic members who oppose abortion, like Tim Ryan from Ohio and Jim Langevin from Rhode Island, have realized that the only way to prevent abortion is to prevent unwanted pregnancy, and they're working with pro-choice legislators to enact comprehensive pregnancy prevention legislation.

Further, Congress needs to redouble its commitment to ethical cell-based research. This, of course, means removing the barriers of President Bush's shortsighted 2001 executive order on embryonic stem cell research—but that's only a place to start. It also means establishing an unbiased, science-based ethics review panel to oversee all cutting edge research, including embryonic, adult, and cord blood stem cell research and SCNT. It means working with individual states that have adopted their own protocols to harmonize the rules so researchers can work with state and federal money. It means banning human reproductive cloning and urging the United Nations and our allies around the world to do the same. And it means making a substantial financial commitment to this exciting new research that could impact so many lives.

The United States also needs to restore reason to its international policies. We must repeal the Mexico City language that prevents the dissemination of birth control devices to poor women around the world. We must stop playing politics with HIV/AIDS prevention policies and allow each country receiving U.S. aid to develop its own comprehensive policies tailored to its culture and health needs, in consultation with experts at international health agencies.

Finally, the American public must stand up and hold its elected officials accountable for letting politics pervade every aspect of public policy relating to reproduction and sex. In my fifteen years in elected office, I have seen the power of the Christian Coalition and its members. While not representative of the views of the majority (or even a large minority) of Americans, this group wields disproportionate influence over our politicians. Why? Because it is a single-issue group that has enormous power to control campaign donations and the votes of its members. If voters who belong to this group are told to denounce a politician because he or she opposes the wishes of this group, they will. No questions asked—and this right here is one of our fundamental problems. I'm afraid *no questions asked* simply doesn't cut it any longer—although I'm not so sure that it ever did.

By contrast, the comparably silent majority of Americans who are pro-research—that's 87 percent of us, by the way—tend not to vote on any one issue. That's why some politicians are motivated to listen to extremists rather than the vast majority. And so, when deciding to support a candidate, voters must not merely investigate his or her position on stem cell research or abortion or even birth control. Voters must do a deeper, more thorough analysis. They must learn where each candidate stands in matters of policy-making and appointment processes as they relate to progressive science.

With John McCain as the presumptive Republican nominee for president in 2008, I believe it's appropriate to examine his views on these important issues. He did, to his credit, vote to expand embryonic stem cell research. On the rest of the issues examined in these pages, though, his record tilts hard right.

For example, in March 2007, a *New York Times* reporter asked Senator McCain the following question: "Should U.S. taxpayer money go to places like Africa to fund contraception to prevent AIDS?"

Senator McCain had obviously not thought at all about the issue, because here's what he replied: "Well, I think it's a combination. The guy I really respect on this is Dr. Coburn."

(Yipes.)

Senator McCain continued: "He [Coburn] believes that you should do what you can to encourage abstinence where there is going to be sexual activity . . . I haven't thought about it. Before

I give you an answer, let me think about it. Let me think about it a little."

Then Senator McCain turned to his press secretary and said, "Get me Coburn's thing. Ask Weaver [the senator's senior adviser, John Weaver] to get me Coburn's paper that he just gave me in the last couple of days. I've never gotten into these issues."

Senator McCain may have never "gotten into these issues," but he sure voted on them. He voted the wrong way on virtually every issue I've discussed in this book. He voted against including birth control in federal employee's health care coverage; he voted against medically accurate pregnancy prevention programs and for abstinence-only programs; he voted to uphold the Mexico City global gag rule; he voted to keep U.S. servicewomen from receiving abortions with their own money at military hospitals abroad; he voted to de-fund the United Nations agency charged with providing family planning services abroad; and on and on.

One of the greatest worries surrounding our choice of president is what he or she will do about judicial appointments—and Senator McCain's record is not encouraging in this respect. While *Roe v. Wade* has been the law of the land for thirty-five years, a lone Supreme Court appointment could overturn that decision and allow states to ban all abortions. Tellingly, Senator McCain has supported four anti-choice U.S. Supreme Court nominees—Justices Alito, Roberts, Thomas, and Bork, who was not confirmed. He also supported six anti-choice lower-court nominees, one of whom also disagreed with a ruling stipulating that insurance companies that offered prescription drug coverage had to also cover contraceptives.

As of this writing, at least, it appears that the McCain agenda on matters of sex and science won't be a whole lot different than the Bush agenda. It looks like we'd be signing on for four more years of more of the same—the same blind faith that dogma and ideology ought to stand ahead of science and reason.

As we sit at the dawn of a new century, it seems almost absurd to be having this discussion. But here we are, having this discussion. Our challenge for the new millennium is to restore reason to our policy-making at the federal level and enact policies that are science-based, compassionate, effective, and sensible. Only then will we be the true stewards of the public trust.

April 2008
Denver, Colorado

INDEX